STARS &
GUITARS

STARS &
GUITARS

MICHAEL HEATLEY

FOREWORD BY BRIAN MAY

$22.95
31994014009853

**CHICAGO
REVIEW
PRESS**

An A Cappella Book

First published in the United States of America in 2010 by
Chicago Review Press, Incorporated
814 North Franklin Street
Chicago, Illinois 60610

© Anova Books 2010

Conceived and produced by
Portico Books, an imprint of Anova Books Company Ltd
10 Southcombe Street
London W14 0RA

ISBN 978-1-56976-535-7

Cover image: Keith Richards courtesy Corbis
Page 2: Billy Joe Armstrong of Green Day courtesy Getty Images

Reproduction by Rival Colour Ltd.
Printed and bound by 1010 Printing International Limited, China

5 4 3 2 1

CONTENTS

FOREWORD

This is the stuff of dreams. I still have a small pile of guitar catalogs that I collected as a boy; looking at them now, I can still feel the excitement and yearning. The pictures show shiny new models from Fender, Gibson, Martin, Selmer, Burns, and others. I dreamed of owning these wonderful instruments and wondered what sounds I would be able to coax from them. My heroes—Rory Gallagher, Hank Marvin, Eric Clapton, and the awesome Jimi Hendrix—wielded these fabulous axes, and we're talking top-of-the-line Stratocasters and Gibson Les Pauls here.

But there was no chance of any of these instruments being within my reach. So it was that I set out to make my own guitar at home with my Dad—a project that lasted about three years of evenings after school. That's the story of how my guitar came about, but in this volume you will find the stories of all my heroes—and yours too. Every guitarist goes through a period of trying things out and then lands up with a guitar and amp setup with which he feels at home—he has found his "voice." The wonderful thing about guitars and guitarists is that EVERY one is different and unique. Here you will find some of the secrets behind many of the world's great guitar-guitarist partnerships—and the kid in all of us can enjoy flicking through, gazing, and dreaming.

Dream on, and enjoy.

Brian May

INTRODUCTION

Few consumer products that were designed and marketed in the late 1940s or early 1950s are still on sale today in their original forms. The one exception to this rule is the electric guitar. Whether a bass, six-string, or twelve-string guitar, the results of Leo Fender and Les Paul's pioneering efforts can still be bought in any guitar shop in the world. Were they both still alive today to be handed one, they'd notice very few changes to the models they developed in the early postwar years, a time when the Space Race had not even begun and when rock 'n' roll was a term Alan Freed had yet to try out on his Moondoggers. The

Slash surrounded by an array of his favorite Gibson Les Pauls.

names they gave their guitars have become legend; the Fender Stratocaster, the Fender Telecaster, and the Gibson Les Paul still dominate the market. In fact, vintage models from the golden age of the 1950s can command impressive prices at auction. Specialist instrument auctioneers Bromptons in West London estimate that a 1958 Stratocaster will sell for more than $30,000, whatever the condition. But not everybody wants to pay the going rate: Rolling Stone Ronnie Wood got so fed up after several of his handmade Zemaitis guitars were stolen that he invited a collector of the brand to tour with him…and bring his guitars for him to use.

A closer look at the axes of choice wielded by rock gods will reveal quite a variety on display—from the angular modernity of Jack White's (White Stripes) National Airline model to the classic lines of Caleb Followill's (Kings of Leon) Gibson ES-325. Both these guitars were designed and built before their players were born. Within these pages you will find guitars from Aria through to the incredibly lovely Zemaitis, choice instruments played by the very best in their profession.

And so, armed with this book, the average rock fan is in the perfect position to become a guitar spotter. Researching it made me even more of one. I've had the privilege of interviewing many talented players from Slash to Steve Vai, and I've also played bass in various bands; however writing this book has added to my knowledge of who played what and when. While checking out the tracks that Brian Jones used his Vox Teardrop on in the early Rolling Stones catalog, I came across footage of one of their first U.S. performances of "Little Red Rooster"—I was surprised to learn that Jones's slide guitar was played on a Vox!

Guitars such as the Teardrop, the Gibson Flying V, or the John Entwistle–inspired Warwick Buzzard are very easy to spot at a distance. But some of the modern guitars that echo the design of the classic Strat can appear a touch more generic—unless of course they come in customized paint schemes, such as those favored by Kirk Hammett of Metallica.

Perhaps one of the reasons that guitar design has remained rooted in its 1950s heritage is the array of effects that guitarists can employ to enhance, expand, and distort their sound. While the guitar may have stayed relatively constant, the armory of effects that a guitarist can plug into is now colossal.

Choosing whom to link to a specific guitar has been the most contentious aspect of this book. Jimi Hendrix is well known for playing a Fender Stratocaster, but including him there would mean losing either Pink Floyd's David Gilmour or Eric Clapton from the roster. That is why you will find Hendrix's name attached to a Flying V—which, to be fair, he customized rather more than most of his Fenders. The ones, at least, he didn't burn or smash.

Guitarists often chop and change their instruments throughout their careers; the more successful they become, the more guitar makers will tailor a product to suit their needs. Few musicians attach themselves to only one model, although there are exceptions: Bruce Springsteen has used the Telecaster for all his "plugged" performances, B. B. King is still married to "Lucille," and Johnny Ramone played nothing but a Mosrite, which perfectly suited the punk ethic. His first cost him $50 and, he said, "was made from really good cardboard." No air guitars were included within these pages, but cardboard just barely qualifies.

Michael Heatley

AMPEG/DAN ARMSTRONG GUITAR
DAVE GROHL

Since abandoning the drum stool with Nirvana to front his own band Foo Fighters, Dave Grohl has shown a consistent liking for retro-styled guitars, realizing how good they look in the videos that enjoy heavy rotation on MTV.

He was doubtless influenced by Rolling Stone Keith Richards's use of the Ampeg/Dan Armstrong guitar in the 1970s, when it was one of the most eye-catching instruments on the block. Richards, traditionally associated with the Telecaster, had a soft spot for his Ampeg, and both he and Bill Wyman played six- and four-string variations on the band's 1969 world tour that spawned the live album *Get Yer Ya-Ya's Out!*

Grohl was first seen playing it on the video for 2002 single "All My Life," after which approving comments from fans flooded the Internet.

Due solely to Grohl's patronage, the Ampeg made the top 25 in *Blender* magazine's 2007 most recognizable guitars poll. Grohl owns four Ampegs that are all tuned differently for various Foo Fighters songs, and at least one of them featured in two more of the Foos' most popular releases: "The One" and "Times Like These."

Notable Ampeg/Dan Armstrong players:
Tom Petty; Jack Bruce; Greg Ginn (Black Flag); Joe Perry; Ronnie Wood; Todd Rundgren.

AMPEG/DAN ARMSTRONG GUITAR

American amplifier manufacturer Ampeg first entered the guitar market in 1963 when, for a year, they offered re-badged Burns guitars (made in the U.K.) to the U.S. market. It proved a short-lived venture. Five years later they reentered the fray when a New York–based guitar repair man named Dan Armstrong designed a range of futuristic-looking see-through Lucite (Perspex) guitars and short-scale basses. These too lasted little more than a year in production, though they have since become collector's items. They featured six different pickups, attached by screws, that could be slid in and out at will; two were supplied with each instrument, the other four being optional add-on purchases.

The double-cutaway guitar failed to attract a wide enough customer base to justify the expense of production. The dense bulletproof material the body was made from was far from cheap. The theory was that the density and uniformity of the material would eliminate unwanted vibrations and frequencies, improving sustain by transferring the string vibrations uninterrupted by any variations in wood grain. Original Ampeg/Dan Armstrongs weighed in at around 15 pounds.

Replicas have recently been made available as the ADA4 (bass) and ADA6 (guitar). The AMG100 is a wooden-bodied variation that gets over the original's weight problem by using ash or alder, but inevitably at the expense of visual impact. These newer examples also had a proper bridge that allowed individual string intonation, as opposed to the rudimentary wood structure of the original. Pickups were now by Dan Armstrong's son Kent, a success story in his own right.

The bass version of the Ampeg/Dan Armstrong is shown here, as played by Bill Wyman and Jack Bruce. Ampeg copies from the 1970s by Ibanez and Shaftesbury are also rare and collectible.

ARIA SB-1000 BASS
BRUCE FOXTON

Bruce Foxton was bass player of the Jam between the mid-1970s and 1982. Since that seminal time in British rock he played with Stiff Little Fingers before celebrating his first band's thirtieth recording anniversary in 2007 in the company of drummer Rick Buckler, albeit without singer-songwriter Paul Weller.

Having started with a Höfner Violin Bass in homage to Paul McCartney, Foxton graduated from a Rickenbacker copy to the real thing. He then switched to a Fender Precision at the time of recording the classic Jam album *All Mod Cons* (1978) in an attempt to obtain a richer tone for his melodic lines.

He moved on to the Japanese-made Aria Pro II SB-1000, and was one of its first

exponents. He used it in the latter days of the Jam and could be seen with it on a farewell tour of the U.K. and events to promote final single "Beat Surrender," notably playing it on the valedictory appearance of the Jam on U.K. TV's *The Tube* in 1982.

He also used it during his short-lived solo career, on the hit single "Freak" and album *Touch Sensitive*, although his bass was far from prominent on the recordings in a very 1980s pop production.

When he started touring in his own tribute band, From the Jam, in 2007, Foxton had reverted to a Precision, and now also plays a Waterstone semi-acoustic.

His amplification setup throughout the Jam years was a Marshall 100-watt bass amplifier with up to four speaker cabinets each containing four 12-inch speakers, the number depending on the size of the venue. This setup suited his toppy tones and upfront lead style of playing.

Notable Aria players: John Taylor (Duran Duran); Jack Bruce; Cliff Burton (Metallica).

ARIA SB-1000 BASS

Founded by classical guitarist Shiro Arai in the 1950s, Japanese manufacturer Arai (later Aria) were one of the first manufacturers of Gibson and Fender copies—a phenomenon that put Japan on the guitar-making map in the late 1960s.

The original designs of the Pro II series, which emerged in 1975, quickly expanded to include basses as well as guitars—the SB-1000 was the top of the Super Bass line and became the most popular bass they ever made.

Introduced in 1980, it was a single-pickup, active instrument with twenty-four frets and neck-through-body construction. It was as expensive as a Fender Jazz, but better built with superior hardware.

The body was made of dark Canadian ash with a walnut strip next to the neck, which was a sandwich of maple-walnut-maple-walnut-maple. The fingerboard was exotic jacaranda, while neck-through-body construction permitted a heel-less cutaway that allowed easy access to the highest frets.

Controls governing the MB-1E double-coil pickup were volume and tone, while a toggle switch turned the battery-powered active circuit on and off. A six-position rotary switch for active tones from the unique BB circuit offered the player amazing sonic flexibility at the turn of a single knob. Each of the six presets changed the frequency of a low pass filter, which radically altered the character of the bass tone. The settings ranged from 1377 Hz, the classic dull, woody 1960s sound (Jack Bruce circa Cream) all the way up to the 186 Hz, a bright, funky tone similar to an Alembic—not surprising as both Jack Bruce and Stanley Clarke, among others, were consulted in the design stages.

The sound was piano-like, with great sustain, while super-quiet electronics on both active and passive settings and zero fret buzz made it ideal for studio use.

Aria basses put Japan on the map in terms of top-line instruments. They used the Matsumoku woodworking factory to make their instruments under contract, and their designer Nobuaki Hayashi designed the SB-1000.

BURNS MARVIN
HANK MARVIN

Hank Marvin, lead guitarist of British instrumental rock pioneers the Shadows, was the man who introduced the U.K. to the Fender Stratocaster, importing the first from the States in the summer of 1959. But Bruce Welch, the group's rhythm guitarist, had an acute sensitivity to pitch, and for him the Strat sometimes proved difficult to tune. Matters came to a head during a 1963 summer season in Blackpool. Marvin said, "Bruce used to throw guitars against the wall. He couldn't handle the tuning situation, he was getting obsessed by it so we decided to change." Marvin suggested they hook up with British guitar designer Jim Burns.

The result was the Burns Marvin, which was played by the group until 1970. The advent of Burns instruments gave the Shadows a whole new sound, as can be heard by comparing the early Fender-created hits like "Apache" and Burns-made music such

BURNS MARVIN

While never as popular as the Stratocaster, the Burns Marvin was in fact a superior instrument. Its construction, circuitry, and scale length of 25.5 inches was similar to the Fender, but it featured Burns's own patented "Rez-o-matik" pickups, mounted at an angle to the strings unlike on the Strat. A three-piece scratchplate topped it off with distinction.

Marvin fed in many of his ideas, including the distinctively scrolled headstock, while fellow Shadow Bruce Welch also had input into the design of the new instrument. Welch's and Marvin's had slightly different pole spacing and pickup positions. This resulted in a sound that was a bit more "nasal," with a more pronounced mid-range.

The guitar's sophisticated vibrato, known as "Rez-o-tube," had six tubes to anchor the strings rather than Fender's single metal block—these resonating tubes being employed to enhance sustain—while the knife-edge bearing on which it swiveled was state of the art. According to Burns's promotional material, the "Marvin" was finished as standard in white, and cost £162 (the luxury case was an additional £14).

The Baldwin Piano and Organ Company would buy Burns in 1965. Since then there have been various relaunches of the line, and instruments such as Korean-made Marquee have proved popular with 1990s groups as much for their retro style as their playability.

Only 300 to 350 Burns Marvins were made in 1964–65, and these are now highly prized by collectors. In 2005 Burns London announced the Shadows Custom Signature, available as a limited edition of 500 guitars with a hand-signed certificate from Marvin and Welch, but these reproductions have had no impact on the value of originals.

While this Burns Marvin reissue, with "autographed" vibrato unit, is fiesta red in emulation of Marvin's iconic Strat, the man himself favored a white finish.

as "Genie with the Light Brown Lamp" and "Don't Make My Baby Blue."

Early problems came when the guitar's vibrato unexpectedly locked out of tune, but then it was discovered that Marvin's jacket button had been getting stuck in a slit in the guitar's back plate covering the springs.

During the same 1964–70 period, Marvin also used the Double Six—a twelve-string guitar popular with the likes of the Searchers—most notably on the intro to Cliff Richard's 1964 hit "On the Beach"; the Shadows did double duty as Cliff's backing band.

The return to Fender was occasioned by the fact that the Shadows had their gear stolen in 1971 and it was never recovered. "I had a dalliance with the Burns for a few years," said Marvin, "but the Strat was my first true love. They're both very good guitars. There is a similarity in the sound... but there is a difference. The Fender is a lighter guitar, a little bit easier to wear on stage. And I prefer the ease of use of the whammy bar on the Fender, which I use a lot."

Notable Burns players include: Andy Bell (Oasis); Gaz Coombes (Supergrass).

CHARVEL FRANKENSTRAT
EDDIE VAN HALEN

When Eddie Van Halen's self-named four-piece burst onto the scene in 1978, lead singer David Lee Roth was of the opinion that "Eddie Van Halen is the first guitar hero of the eighties; all the other guitar heroes are dead."

Van Halen's sound and style came courtesy of a homemade guitar he'd fashioned from $130 worth of parts and known as "Godzilla" or, sometimes, "Frankenstrat." His first original instrument had been a 1958 Fender Stratocaster, but band members felt its single-coil pickups didn't give him a meaty enough sound. A semi-acoustic Gibson ES-335

came closer but failed on image grounds. Besides, Eddie soon found he was missing the Strat's whammy bar. So Godzilla it was, and with a single humbucking pickup—a Gibson angled to align the pole pieces with the thinner, Fender-style string spacing—near the bridge and just one knob (a volume control), the instrument was simplicity itself.

Van Halen's red, white and black splatter-striped color scheme was achieved with Schwinn bicycle paint, and is so associated with him it was trademarked in 2001.

Godzilla was the means by which Van Halen obtained his "brown sound—big, warm and majestic." His father Jan was a saxophone player, and Van Halen has since suggested he was trying to create a hornlike tone. "If you can get a real, sweet distortion to it, you can make it sound like a sax." The success of Van Halen delighted Dad, though "I think deep down he wanted us to be a little more respectable."

Van Halen used the homemade axe extensively on the band's 1978 eponymous first album and on the road, while his other studio guitar was an Ibanez Destroyer similar to those endorsed by Kiss. He plugged his guitars into a 100-watt Marshall Super Lead amp with a Plexi front that dated from 1967; it has made an appearance on every Van Halen album since. Flange and phase effects, where used, were operated by a footswitch as onstage—a practice that would give current producers apoplexy.

CHARVEL FRANKENSTRAT

Wayne Charvel had started his company in 1974 as purely a component and kit manufacturer, supplying guitarists from his base in northern Los Angeles. After Eddie Van Halen found fame with a "bitsa" built from a Charvel-supplied body and neck, among other components, Charvel started marketing complete guitars. By this time, however, he had run into financial problems and handed over control to an employee, Grover Jackson.

Van Halen's model was never explicitly manufactured at the time, but he lent his name to the MusicMan EVH from January 1990 to late 1995 (after which it reverted to being the Axis) and then a similar guitar manufactured by Peavey.

In 2004 Eddie began to sell his own design of Charvel guitars called "EVH Art Series Guitars" modeled after his earlier "Frankenstrat" guitars, right down to the volume pot being replaced with a tone knob just like the original! These featured custom-striped basswood bodies, a special-wound humbucking pickup, original Floyd Rose tremolo, and a compound-radius maple neck carved from his original specs. This curved dramatically at the nut for easy chording, flattening out as it approached the neck joint for low-action bends without fretting out (that is, bending the string without colliding with the frets).

These guitars were made available in a choice of three color variations: white with black stripes, black with yellow stripes, and red with black and white stripes.

The chaotic appearance of Eddie Van Halen's "Frankenstrat" at close quarters reflects his constant tinkering with pickups to obtain maximum tone. Note the way the humbucker is angled to the strings.

DANELECTRO 59-DC
JIMMY PAGE

The Danelectro (Dano) make was a cheap alternative to "name" guitars introduced in the 1950s with budget-conscious postwar kids in mind, yet interest shown in the following decade from top players like Jimmy Page upped its profile and desirability.

Page used a black double-cutaway Danelectro (Model 3021, later reissued as 59-DC Standard and 59-DC Pro) as a slide guitar from the early Led Zeppelin days of the late 1960s, wearing a bottleneck on his ring finger. The guitar's bright tone favored this technique, which was pioneered by the veteran bluesmen from whom Zeppelin took inspiration.

Such cheap guitars lent themselves to risk-free modification. Page fitted a metal bridge to his sometime prior to 1975 to replace the original rudimentary wooden example. In any case, his black Dano with white pickguard was already a hybrid, having been made from the best parts of two different instruments.

The result can be heard on "In My Time of Dying." Other songs for which it was used onstage include "Babe I'm Gonna Leave You," "White Summer/Black Mountain Side," and "Kashmir."

There are two models of the Danelectro 59-DC, the Standard and the Pro. The Standard is the model that

DANELECTRO 59-DC

The Danelectro company was originally founded in the postwar years by Nathan Daniel as an amplifier manufacturer and went on to sell many of its guitars via Sears department stores. Silvertones were initially distinguishable by having different-shaped headstocks, but the Silvertone's "Coke bottle" shape was eventually adopted throughout.

Danelectros were of deliberately cheap construction—their bodies weren't even made wholly of wood. A poplar wood frame that comprised the sides, neck, and bridge block of the guitar was stapled together and covered with 0.4-inch thick Masonite (a kind of hardboard). The top and back were painted, but the sides were covered in a vinyl material to hide the unpainted wood frame. Another feature was their distinctive pickup covers, which were actually surplus chrome-plated lipstick tubes.

The two-pickup 3021 is considered the Jimmy Page model, with its seal-shaped pickguard and concentric knobs for

volume and tone. However, contrary to logic, the wider, dark-colored control is the volume control, and the cream-colored, smaller top knob is the tone control. There is also a three-way pickup selector switch, which permits users to choose either pickup alone or both pickups together.

The first chapter of the Danelectro story ended in 1969 when new owners MCA cut their losses. A revived range of Dano classics was offered for sale in the late 1990s, as well as new designs such as the asymmetrical, Mosrite-inspired Hodad, but the revivals failed to sell in appreciable quantities.

Reissues of the 59-DC and other Danelectros can be distinguished by a chunk cut out of the distinctive "Coke bottle" headstock to avoid deception when being sold.

Squint at the Danelectro's white pickguard and the profile of a seal becomes apparent—just one of the instrument's many idiosyncrasies.

Jimmy Page plays, and it has a painted neck. The 59-DC Standard does not have a bridge with adjustable saddles, so the musician cannot adjust the intonation of each string. Page's alteration made it more like a 59-DC Pro, which has a fully adjustable bridge.

Interestingly, the Danelectro that Page favored was made in the same year as the

Gibson Les Paul, which he used as his main instrument in the Zeppelin years. Needless to say, the values of the two guitars differ wildly.

Notable Danelectro players: Syd Barrett (Pink Floyd); Jimi Hendrix, whose second guitar ever was a Dano.

DANELECTRO LONG HORN BASS
GARRY TALLENT

With their exaggerated body styles, Danelectro's Long Horn guitars and basses were some of the late 1950s' and 1960s' most visually distinctive instruments. The Long Horn bass enjoyed a spell in the spotlight when played by Garry Tallent, who used it as his main instrument in the early years backing Bruce Springsteen in the E Street Band.

The instrument was a logical choice, as Danelectros were built in Neptune City, New Jersey, from 1958 onwards. Rumor has it that Tallent himself worked at the factory and put together at least one of the instruments he used personally. He had played the tuba before the bass, so the Dano would not have been too user-unfriendly for a nonguitarist to master.

Its crisp, cutting tone can be heard in live and studio recordings from that era—the title

DANELECTRO LONG HORN BASS

Made of Masonite, with sides of poplar or pine covered with vinyl, the Long Horn bass was introduced around 1958. These distinctive instruments came in four- and six-string versions (Danelectro had produced the first ever six-string bass, the UB-1, in 1955).

The new offering's 29.5-inch short scale and almost completely flat fingerboard made playing easy for bassists intimidated by Fender's regulation 34-inch scale. It was also friendlier to guitarists converting to a new instrument. There were twenty-four frets, though the more conservatively styled Short Horn, introduced in 1959, had just fifteen.

Nathan Daniel explained the concept thus: "The idea was simply to give the players as much access [to the fretboard]

as possible, which meant that instead of a single cutaway we had a deep cutaway on both sides. It did make an unusual look, sure, but it was an unusual name too: a couple of long horns."

Sound-wise, the Long Horn had a surprisingly full, resonant bass tone, undoubtedly due in part to the semihollow body. The unusual control setup means the stacked knobs are not the expected volume and tone controls. The wedge-shaped top knobs are simply on/off switches for each pickup, and the bottom round knobs are volume only.

Although the brand name has been revived, the era of "true" Danelectros ended long ago. Nashville guitar maker Jerry Jones has made Dano-inspired basses and guitars for many years, and his dedication is testament to the marque's value and enduring appeal.

From left to right: Bruce Springsteen, Steven Van Zandt, and Garry Tallent.

The plastic-headed tuners and strap locks are often upgraded, but in most other respects the Danelectro Long Horn is perfectly giggable— even at the size of venue the E Street Band is used to playing.

cut of "Born to Run" is the most famous example, but other early tracks, like the first album's "Incident on 57th Street" and the long-unreleased song "Fire," are also of note. Tallent took three of these basses on the E Street Band's 1999 Reunion Tour, one of which was the same instrument he played on "Born to Run."

During the period the E Street Band was inactive, Tallent moved to Nashville, having an affinity for country and western and rockabilly music. He donated his most famous Long Horn bass, in white sunburst finish (bronze sunburst was the other available option), to the city's Musicians Hall of Fame and Museum, which opened in June 2006.

Tallent resurrected the Long Horn when Springsteen and the E Street Band reconvened, playing it on "Waiting on a Sunny Day" from 2002's *The Rising*, the first full-length studio album they had released in eighteen years.

Notable Danelectro bass players:
John Entwistle (The Who); Jack Bruce; LA/Nashville session musician Richard Bennett.

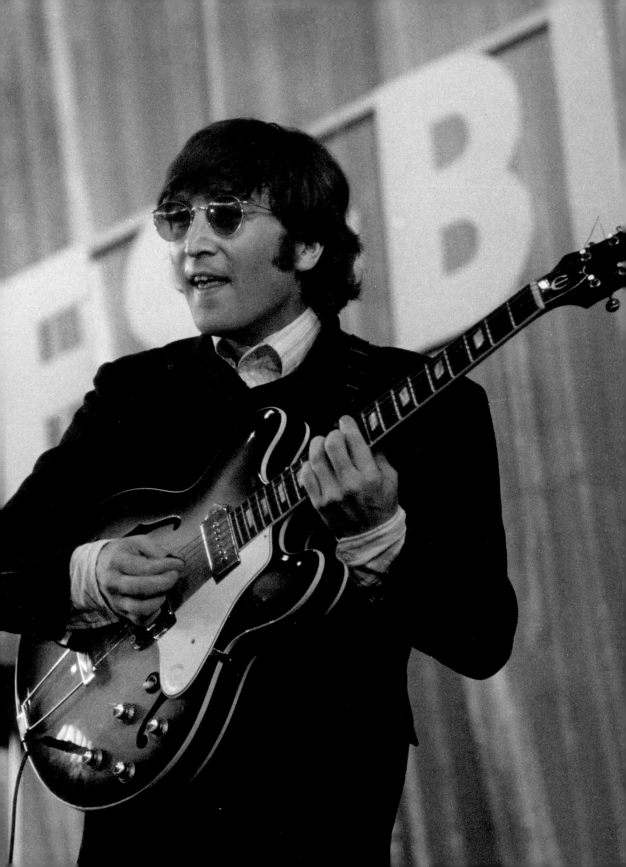

EPIPHONE CASINO
JOHN LENNON

Beatles John Lennon, Paul McCartney, and George Harrison each owned a Casino.

Lennon first used it live in May 1966 at the New Musical Express Poll-Winners' Concert at London's Empire Pool. His Casino and his Gibson J-160E acoustic featured throughout the sessions for *Revolver*, and it is the guitar he played and was pictured with for the last half of the Beatles' recording career.

After their visit to India in 1968 to study meditation, the Beatles had the finish professionally removed from several instruments at Donovan's suggestion, including Lennon's Casino. He had spray painted its back and neck with white and gray psychedelic designs in 1967. The pickguard was removed during the *Sgt. Pepper* recording sessions, leaving the mounting bracket and screw on the guitar, but the guard was never replaced. At one point a black replacement knob took the place of a missing gold original.

Filming for what was to become the movie *Let It Be* started in January 1969 and the Casino featured throughout. Post-Beatles, Lennon continued to use it both live and in the studio with the Plastic Ono Band, changing the stock Epiphone tuning pegs to a set of gold Grovers.

Two Limited Edition John Lennon Casinos have been made available by Gibson/Epiphone.

> **Notable Epiphone Casino players:**
> Johnny Marr (the Smiths); Tom Petty; Brian Jones and Keith Richards; Dave Davies (the Kinks); Carl Wilson and Al Jardine (the Beach Boys); Lee Ranaldo (Sonic Youth); singer-songwriter Matthew Sweet.

EPIPHONE CASINO

The Epiphone Casino is a hollow-bodied electric guitar first made in 1958 and, as with most of the company's products, is a "licensed copy" based on a Gibson design—in this case the ES-330 series. It is fitted with P-90 pickups and, unlike most hollow-bodied electric guitars, doesn't have a center block. This combination of build and pickup type means it is lighter and louder but also more prone to feedback.

The body of the Casino is made of laminated maple and the neck is mahogany, although it has occasionally been maple. The fretboard is either rosewood or ebony, depending on the model, with parallelogram inlays. The first versions had a spruce top but subsequent models, until 1970, had a headstock made of five laminated layers of maple and birch; the headstock was set at a 17-degree angle. Since then, the headstock has been set at a 14-degree angle and the top, along with the sides and back, has consisted of five layers of maple laminate.

The manufacturing of the Casino moved from Korea to China in 2007. So-called USA-Collection Epiphones are assembled in the United States from components manufactured in Japan; this line includes two John Lennon signature models.

Lennon had planned to restore his Casino to its original sunburst, but the refinishing never took place. It is now on display at the John Lennon Museum in Saitama, Japan.

EPIPHONE SHERATON/ SUPERNOVA
NOEL GALLAGHER

Since John Lennon and Paul McCartney were fans of semi-acoustic Epiphone guitars, it was no surprise when Noel Gallagher, lead guitarist of Beatles-influenced Oasis, adopted one as his main stage guitar in the 1990s. The Epiphone Riviera that Gallagher and guitar partner Paul "Bonehead" Arthurs used were made in Japan by the Matsumoko factory from around 1978 to 1982; these differ from other Riviera models in having humbuckers and stop-tail bridges.

Gallagher further enhanced the Epiphone-brand profile when he commissioned a Sheraton with a Union Jack graphic. This guitar went well onstage with his parka-clad "mod" image and made its debut at Manchester City FC's Maine Road ground, where the group played in 1996. It was customized by a London luthier and featured a Frequensator tailpiece and Alnico-V minihumbucker pickups.

Its maple neck boasted split-parallelogram inlays while on the headstock was a Gibsonesque diamond. The distinctive pickguard acquired a signature alongside the iconic brand symbol. A laminated maple body and chrome hardware completed the guitar.

The Sheraton held sway between 1996 and 2000, replacing the Epiphone Les Paul as his chosen axe. Since 2002, Gallagher's primary stage instruments have been a Bigsby-equipped cherry Gibson ES-355, a burgundy 1972 Epiphone Riviera, and an Epiphone Sheraton in tobacco sunburst.

Noel Gallagher's signature guitar, the Epiphone Supernova, is supposedly based on the Sheraton but is entirely different from the Union Jack guitar played at Maine Road. It has a stop-tail bridge and humbuckers as opposed to a Frequensator and minihumbuckers, making it closer to the Epiphone Sheraton II or the 1970s Epiphone Riviera. Introduced in 1997 and named after the Oasis song "Champagne Supernova," it was available in the light blue of Noel's favorite soccer team, Manchester City.

Notable Epiphone Sheraton players:
John Lee Hooker; Matthew Followill (Kings of Leon).

EPIPHONE SHERATON

Gibson bought the Epiphone company in 1957 to make second-line instruments such as the Crestwood, Coronet, and Century, but the Sheraton semi-acoustic, developed in 1958, was very much a prestige guitar.

It was introduced after the Century arch-top guitar had been fitted with a P-90 pickup and proved a popular upmarket alternative, and was the second most expensive f-hole guitar in the range. It had twin humbuckers and double cutaways, which made it not dissimilar to the Gibson 335 in appearance.

It had a laminated maple body with a solid maple block down the center of the body to minimize feedback; combined with the hollow wings, this gave good sustain, tone, and weight. The Sheraton featured a three-piece maple neck with rosewood fingerboard and block and triangle inlays instead of Gibson's usual dot, block, or double trapezoids. The large headstock with an inlaid tree motif was another distinguishing feature.

While Gibson's 335 usually featured a stop-tail or, in some cases, a vibrato tailpiece, the Sheraton had an old-fashioned Frequensator trapeze. The Epiphone Sheraton II was later introduced and replaced the Frequensator by a fixed stop-tail. A Bigsby vibrato tailpiece was optional.

In 1961 Sheratons began to use Gibson-made parts. The pickups became minihumbuckers, knobs became gold Gibson knobs, and tuners became Grovers. Necks were no longer made in New York by Epiphone but were Gibson mahogany necks. The peghead was also elongated. By 1970 the guitar was no longer made in the United States and was promoted as a reissue.

Noel Gallagher's Union Jack Sheraton was a present from his then girlfriend Meg Mathews. While he played the original without a pickguard, replicas (right) bore his embossed signature.

ESP
KIRK HAMMETT

Kirk Hammett, lead guitarist of metal megaband Metallica, has employed a variety of ESP instruments, all with customized paint jobs and special features. Hammett began his association with the company after recording and touring the *Master of Puppets* album in 1986, and the relationship continues to this day. The ESP guitars replaced old faithfuls—a black Jackson Randy Rhoads Custom (known to its owner as "the shark fin guitar"), a similarly colored Fernandes Stratocaster, and a Gibson Flying V.

Hammett and ESP's company president Matt Masciandaro have worked together closely over the past decade to assemble a range of guitars built to his specifications. The marque was used extensively when recording the album *And Justice for All* in 1988, and since then they have been the Metallica axe of choice.

And Justice for All featured Hammett's original ESP MII. The headstock is slightly different from those that followed; the side of the headstock is flat on this guitar, while later examples are flat at the top. Also, the skull inlays on this first ESP are oriented differently, running up and down when the guitar is in its stand rather than when it is actually being played. This guitar now resides at the Rock and Roll Hall of Fame in Cleveland, Ohio.

The more famous of Hammett's guitars are all KH-2s built or overseen by Matt Masciandaro. They are named "Ouiji," "The Mummy," "Caution," and "Spider," and bear fantasy artwork appropriate to their names.

The Black Album of 1991 (actually titled *Metallica*) saw three ESP guitars used: the

ESP

Japanese firm ESP (Electric Sound Products) are famed for being the choice of many thrash-metal players. ESP first enjoyed success making bodies and necks for Kramer, Robin, Schecter Guitar Research, and DiMarzio. Then they graduated to making complete guitars and prospered in the early 2000s after Fender bought out Jackson, their nearest rivals, and many high-profile players switched to them.

A Superstrat with reverse headstock, the M-250 is similar in shape to Ibanez, and ESP have run into problems with Gibson and PRS for moving too close to their designs. The range of model numbers is exceptionally confusing, with the initial letter representing the body shape (for example, "M" for "Mirage"). Kirk Hammett's first ESP was an MII.

The KH series of guitar are maple-neck through-body designs with alder bodies and rosewood fretboards. All hardware (Tune-o-matic bridges, stop piece, Floyd Rose bridges and arms, and tuners) comes in standard black. Most have Fender-style three-way slot switches, two volume controls (one for each pickup), and one tone.

In 1996, ESP started a new brand, LTD, whose guitars are similar to the higher-end ESP guitars but are more affordable and cater mainly to markets outside of Japan. ESP also market a couple of affordable KH models that are less than $1,000.

While bearing his signature on the headstock, replica Kirk Hammett guitars were not always as colorful as the originals ("Ouija" is pictured far right).

KH-1 named "Devil" was a Flying V-style instrument while "Skull and Crossbones II" and "Ouija" were twin humbucker KH-2 designs based on the MII.

The KH-4 has been modeled after a Gibson of which Hammett is particularly fond. All in all, nearly twenty variations of the ESP Kirk Hammett existed in 2010.

Notable ESP players: Vernon Reid (Living Colour); Vinnie Vincent and Bruce Kulick (Kiss); Ronnie Wood (the Rolling Stones). Other users include Hammett's Metallica colleague James Hetfield, whose "Truckster" was introduced into ESP's Signature Series in 2005 to celebrate the company's thirtieth anniversary.

FENDER FRETLESS JAZZ BASS
JACO PASTORIUS

American bass virtuoso Jaco Pastorius first came to public attention in 1976 when he joined jazz-rock fusionists Weather Report. He succeeded two gifted yet contrasting bass players, Miroslav Vitous and Alphonso Johnson, and arrived in time to play on the 1976 release *Black Market*. His six-year spell in the ranks saw the band enjoy its greatest commercial success with the single "Birdland."

Pastorius had trained as a drummer but switched from drums to bass in his teens because he broke his arm in an accident. He bought a Fender Jazz Bass in Florida for $90 in the early 1970s and soon became the world's leading fretless player. In 1978, Pastorius told luthier Kevin Kaufman that he removed the frets himself using a butter knife, filling the fret slots with plastic and wood and applying several coats of epoxy.

Kaufman replaced the peeling epoxy by pouring on a single coat and shaping it with a rasp. In the mid-1980s, when Pastorius smashed the bass in an argument, Kaufman and fellow repairman Jim Hamilton glued together fifteen large and several small pieces and laminated a maple veneer to keep the body together.

Aside from Weather Report, Joni Mitchell allowed Pastorius another context in which to display his brilliance on her albums *Hejira* (the title track in particular) and *Mingus*. Pastorius's eponymous solo album—released in 1976, the twenty-fifth anniversary of the introduction of the Fender Bass—became a touchstone for a generation of players. "Portrait of Tracy," played almost exclusively with natural harmonics, remains today a test for any would-be fretless bassist to measure his or her abilities. The "Jaco growl" is obtained by using the bridge pickup exclusively and plucking the strings right above it.

Pastorius's life was to end prematurely and senselessly in 1987 after a barroom brawl.

As Toto founder-member David Hungate, now a Nashville session ace, put it, "No other individual has so totally revolutionized and expanded the approach to an instrument."

Joe Zawinul, cofounder of Weather Report, was of the same opinion. "I heard him play only four bars and I knew history was being made," he recalled after the first time they played together.

Both of Pastorius's Fender basses—the other a 1960 fretted Jazz—were stolen in 1986. In 1993, the fretted bass resurfaced in a New York City music shop. In 2008, the 1962 fretless "Bass of Doom" also turned up in New York.

Notable Fender Fretless Jazz Bass players: Tony Franklin, who has his own signature Precision.

FENDER FRETLESS JAZZ BASS

The Fender Jazz Bass has a narrower neck than its older brother the Precision, making it easier and faster to play. Its hybrid tone combines the ability of an upright bass to allow seamless slides and the softer edges of notes that only an instrument without metal frets can provide, with the up-front presence of an amplified electric bass. Rolling off the neck pickup and soloing the bridge is the key to obtaining classic fretless growl that can be heard through all but the thickest instrumentation.

Playing a fretless instrument usually requires much more training of the fretting hand for exact positioning and shifts and more ear training to discern the minute differences in intonation that fretless instruments permit. To make this easier, many fretless guitars and basses have lines in place of frets and side position markers (dots or lines), indicating halftone increments.

On fretless basses the fingerboard is usually made of a hard wood, such as ebony. To reduce fingerboard wear from roundwound strings, a coat of epoxy may be applied. Other strings, such as flatwound, groundwound, or nylon tapewound strings, can also be used to reduce fingerboard wear; on a fretted bass, contact is made with the metal frets rather than the wooden fingerboard.

In 1999, the Fender Custom Shop made available a Jaco Pastorius Jazz, replicating his road-weary instrument in every detail down to the removed pickguard.

Remove the pickguard and frets from a Fender Jazz Bass and you too can play like Jaco Pastorius. Note the grounding strip between pickup and bridge, a feature of early Jazzes that the original (left) appears to lack.

FENDER JAG-STANG
KURT COBAIN

Like Jimi Hendrix, Kurt Cobain was another southpaw to emerge from Seattle, one who fronted a three-piece band and died too soon. Cobain left a mark on rock music far in excess of the four albums released during his lifetime. Since the release of *Nevermind* in 1991, bands and albums have been classified as pre- or post-Nirvana.

In theory, Cobain would be the least likely guitarist to be attracted by the prospect of a "signature model," yet it was something he positively relished. "I like the idea of having a quality instrument on the market with no preconceived notions attached....I'm the anti-guitar hero—I can barely play the thing." The result was the Jag-Stang.

The no-longer-produced entry-level Fender Mustang had become his unlikely stage favorite because, in his words, "they're cheap and totally inefficient, they sound like crap and are very small." But necessity proved the mother of invention as the combination of the Mustang's short (24-inch) scale and heavy strings helped create his sound.

When the grunge-genre-launching *Nevermind* and the single "Smells Like Teen Spirit" were a success, he engaged Danny Ferrington of the Fender Custom Shop to find him left-handed necks to

FENDER JAG-STANG

Fender's classic trio of Tele, Strat, and Precision proved impossible to top. The Jaguar, Jazzmaster, and Jazz Bass all failed to prove as popular, while entry-level instruments like the Duo-Sonic and Musicmaster, introduced during the 1950s, found only limited acceptance.

Though John Frusciante tackled much of his solo and Red Hot Chili Peppers work with a Jaguar, it was a surprise when early in the 1990s, Kurt Cobain created a signature model from a Jaguar and a Mustang (a Duo-Sonic with vibrato). In a now-famous design exercise, he took Polaroid photos of the guitars, cut them in half, and stuck them together. The result, which he faxed to Fender, was named the Jag-Stang. (In fact, the division is not exactly fifty-fifty.)

The instrument's body was made of basswood, with a maple neck and rosewood fretboard. The neck pickup was a single-coil Fender Texas Special, originally designed as a bridge pickup for Fender's Stevie Ray Vaughan model, with a DiMarzio humbucker at the neck. Three-position slide switches offered many options, including out-of-phase pickups, while a vibrato system was offered. This is surprising, since Cobain thought these "totally worthless: only Jimi Hendrix was able to use the standard tremolo and still keep it in tune. I do have one on a Japanese Strat, but I don't use it."

Japanese-made models of the Jag-Stang hit the market eighteen months after his 1994 death with the approval of Cobain's estate. Fender's Joe Carducci felt it would appeal to "a guitarist with an untraditional attitude who desires an instrument with tone that speaks traditionally." It was discontinued in mid-2001 but has since been reintroduced due to public demand. The rear of the headstock still bears the "Designed by Kurt Cobain" transfer.

Discard the tremolo arm, which Cobain never used—he plays a hard-tail Mustang (far right)—and the Jag-Stang is a usable instrument for all kinds of rock.

replace the ones he destroyed onstage. The next stop, said Ferrington, was to assemble "a more sophisticated Mustang." Ferrington's custom-made Mustang "copy" was used on the *In Utero* sessions, alongside Cobain's favorite electric, a Jaguar, which remained safely studio-bound.

When it came to effects, Cobain claimed to wear out four or five Roland EF-1 distortion boxes per tour, while amplification varied. *In Utero* saw him utilizing a Fender Quad Reverb with three or four power tubes out of action, while an echo flanger was in evidence. Onstage he'd use a PA amp for a guitar head.

Cobain requested two Jag-Stangs, one in Solid Blue and one in Fiesta Red. Only the blue instrument had been delivered before Cobain's death, and was used on Nirvana's 1993 tour.

FENDER JAZZ BASS
GEDDY LEE

Geddy Lee formed the Canadian prog-rock band Rush in 1969 with guitarist Alex Lifeson and drummer John Rutsey (replaced by Neil Peart). They were unashamedly influenced by Cream.

He played a Fender Precision Bass on his first local gigs and on Rush's eponymous debut album, released by Canadian label Moon Records in 1974. And while he's since flirted with Rickenbacker basses, particularly the 4001 model, the headless Steinberger, and British Wal basses, his main squeeze has always been the Fender Jazz.

He found his early-1970s Jazz (either 1972 or 1973—sources vary) in a pawnshop in Kalamazoo, Michigan, and its bright sound has often been mistaken for a Rickenbacker. "I hit the strings so hard," he says, "you can hear not only the frets whack but sometimes the string hitting the pickup!" He will also often tune the

FENDER JAZZ BASS

While the Jazz Bass failed to eclipse its older brother the Precision in the Fender hierarchy, its introduction in 1959 gave the world an instrument that was more sophisticated, having neck and bridge pickups as opposed to the Precision's single unit. Its name by no means designated the only music it was most suitable or for which it was used.

The Jazz featured a pair of pickups resembling the pre-1957 Precision's original straight-across style, while the body was offset to resemble the newly introduced Jazzmaster six-string—hence, perhaps, the choice of name. The Jazz Bass neck was significantly narrower at the nut (headstock end) with a measurement of 1.4 inches, giving a radically different feel to the Precision's 1.75-inch neck. This made it more attractive to guitar players who wished to switch to four strings.

Early Jazz Basses had two concentric, "stacked pot" control knobs, each controlling the volume and tone of their respective pickup. By 1962, however, the still-current three-knob design had been adopted, which added a separate and all-governing potentiometer that cut the treble response of each pickup. Blending the two pickups, however, offered a surprising range of sounds. The one nearer the bridge added a distinctive "honk" to the sound, while the mellow neck pickup was more akin to the Precision's warm tone. Each pickup's volume knob determined how much it contributed to the overall sound.

More sophisticated variations of the Jazz Bass have included five-string and active electronic versions; for the fretless Jazz see pages 30–31. The most profound example of its effect may be seen in the likes of Sandberg, Lakland, and numerous other high-end copies of what has become the classic electric bass design.

The five-string Jazz pictured here lacks the Geddy Lee signature's maple neck with black blocks and heavy-duty Leo Quan Badass replacement bridge.

low E down to a D, while in the concept piece *2112* the whole band detunes a tone, "giving a heavier, darker vibe."

This Jazz Bass can be heard on the albums *Permanent Waves* (1980), *Moving Pictures* (1981), and *Signals* (1982), as well as on their supporting tours. He returned to the instrument when recording *Counterparts* in 1993 and has been using it virtually exclusively since, on albums *Test for Echo*, *Vapor Trails*, *Feedback*, and *Snakes & Arrows*.

Lee liked it so much that he endorsed a signature Jazz that is available to the public and made in Japan. It is modeled on his favorite instrument and features black inlays stenciled on a maple neck (older Jazzes feature pearloid inlays) and a heavy Badass bridge to enhance sustain. The only body color is black, while the artist's signature is on the rounded part of the headstock.

He has also used a Fender Jaco Pastorius Tribute fretless bass and a Fender Custom Shop Jazz with an alder body on tour, the latter in an alternate tuning.

Notable Fender Jazz Bass players: Noel Redding (the Jimi Hendrix Experience); Adam Clayton (U2); Timothy B. Schmitt (Eagles); John Paul Jones (Led Zeppelin).

FENDER JAZZMASTER
TOM VERLAINE

Guitarist Tom Verlaine cofounded art-punk group Television in New York in 1973 with bassist Richard Hell. Hell left two years later to join the Heartbreakers and, later, the Voidoids, leaving Verlaine the undisputed leader.

It was the interlocking guitars of Verlaine and Richard Lloyd that provided the band with their musical trademark. Television's first single, "Little Johnny Jewel," saw Verlaine plugging his Jazzmaster straight into the recording desk with no amplification. Swimming against the prevailing tradition of rock guitar, he rarely used distortion.

After a flirtation with the surf boom, the Jazzmaster had faded from sight until Elvis Costello was featured with one on the cover of his 1977 debut album, *My Aim Is True*. Then came Verlaine.

He explained his choice of guitar as financial. "Nobody wanted a Jazzmaster because they weren't loud and didn't stay in tune. In 1973 and 1974 you could buy a Jazzmaster for $150 easily. So that's why I started playing it."

Verlaine uses a thin pick and heavy strings (gauges .013 to 050) with a wound third and tunes down a half step or more. Verlaine usually plays with the bridge pickup on but picks over the neck pickup.

Television's debut album, *Marquee Moon* (1977), was hailed by critics as a classic, but the band split after the disappointing follow-up, *Adventure* (1978). They reformed in 1992 for a third, eponymously titled album and have performed together occasionally since.

> **Notable Jazzmaster players:** In 2008 Verlaine took part in the Fender Fiftieth Anniversary Jazzmaster concert in New York, featuring Sonic Youth's Thurston Moore and J. Mascis of Dinosaur Jr., two more players who brought the guitar back to relative popularity in the late 1980s and early 1990s.

FENDER JAZZMASTER

Few guitars have gone in and out of fashion as rapidly as the Jazzmaster. Fender's classic trio of Telecaster, Stratocaster, and Precision bass remain their bestsellers today. The Jazzmaster, introduced in 1958 as the top-of-the-range addition to Fender's catalog, was too specialized to pose a major threat.

As its name suggested, the Jazzmaster's major market was jazz guitarists. It was intended as a solid-body alternative to the hollow-body arch-top guitars, mostly Gibsons, that were then ubiquitous. Indeed, the contoured offset-waist body was designed for playing in a seated position, as many jazz and blues artists preferred.

The sound was mellower than the Strat, thanks to white soap-bar-style pickups whose flat and wide coils, in contrast to Fender's usual tall and thin coils, gave a warmer tone without losing clarity. The Jazzmaster was the first Fender guitar to feature a separate rosewood fingerboard, glued on to a maple neck.

The Jazzmaster was officially discontinued in 1980, although guitars sold from 1978 to 1980 were previously produced stock. The Jazzmaster was reintroduced in 1986 as a reissue from Fender's Japanese factory, and an American Vintage Series version was introduced in 1999. An Elvis Costello signature model was also offered by the company.

Though it appears to have been disconnected on this occasion (left), Tom Verlaine's style makes extensive use of the Jazzmaster's tremolo (below).

FENDER PRECISION BASS

LONG-SCALE

The Fender Precision Bass owed its name to the fact that it had frets and so could easily be played with accuracy, unlike the acoustic basses it sought to replace. In 1951, the year of its introduction, the bass sound was felt as much as heard, but it did much to change that situation. The electric guitar was proving impossible for the "doghouse" bass to keep up with, both in speed of playing and volume.

Elvis Presley bassist Bill Black used one in the 1957 movie *Jailhouse Rock*, and its popularity was thereafter assured. Amplification would change the role of the bassist and, in allowing musicians' contributions to be more easily heard, speed the move toward rock music.

The scale length of the Precision was 34 inches, which would become known as long-scale as opposed to medium (32 inches) and short (30 inches). Twenty frets were inlaid on a one-piece maple neck that was bolted to an ash body. A large scratch plate extending all over the top and bottom horns was an identifying feature, with a single-coil pickup being controlled by volume and tone mounted on a chromed plate. A rudimentary two-saddle bridge allowed some basic intonation, though as each saddle served two strings a compromise had to be reached.

ELECTRIC VERSUS ACOUSTIC

The new design offered several advantages: it was a sixth of the size of an acoustic bass and therefore more portable; it was easier for guitarists to transfer to if they wanted to increase employment opportunities; and it was affordable at just less than $200. The E–A–D–G tuning, an octave below the guitar and identical to the acoustic bass, would become the electric bass norm.

The top of the body was extended into a horn— a departure from Telecaster design—to balance the instrument, which had a longer neck and larger tuning keys. Gibson answered the Precision in 1953 with their first electric bass, but they would never catch up.

TELECASTER STYLING

The Fender Precision bass was introduced in 1951 and went on to become an industry standard. Its original Telecaster-style body, made of ash or alder, was

modified in 1957 to reflect the smoother lines of the Stratocaster. The headstock also became fatter and more Strat-shaped, while the original straight-across pickup became a split-coil unit.

A "belly cut," or curved top-body edge, had already been incorporated and the new design retained this comfort option; but while the strings had passed through the body before, they were now anchored behind the bridge.

A maple fretboard, favored by some players for a smoother action, gave way in 1959 to the darker rosewood, but both options became available from 1967 and remain so today. With one-piece maple necks, the truss rod is inserted from the back of the neck and the resulting gouge filled in by a "skunk stripe" of darker wood. A gold anodized scratchplate was briefly standard issue, but as different body colors were introduced, white, black, tortoiseshell, and other variations were offered.

FAVORED MODS

The Precision still looks today as it did in the late 1950s. That said, bassists sometimes get their guitar technicians to add a single-coil Jazz Bass–style pickup between the bridge and the existing pickup to offer the best of both worlds. Active electronic options have been offered by Fender but rarely proved popular.

Precisions were originally supplied with a chrome pickup guard and a similar "ashtray" to shield the bridge. Like the finger rest, these are usually lost or discarded by the user. A foam mute would often be inserted under the bridge unit to muffle the sound.

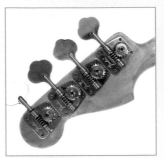

Headstock (left) and array of Precision Basses (below). Fender have made available a Japanese-crafted reproduction of Sting's 1953 Precision with a block signature inlay at the twelfth fret.

The Fender P-Bass in Arctic White. In 2010 it was available in 37 different colors across eight series: Standard, American Deluxe, American Standard, American Vintage, Highway One, Classic, Deluxe, and Road Worn series.

FENDER PRECISION BASS
STING

Bassist/vocalist Sting (real name Gordon Sumner), found fame with the Police playing rock, despite a love of complex jazz. He played many different basses during his Police career, two early examples being Precisions: an orange-colored fretted and a natural maple-bodied fretless. The former can be heard on the breakthrough single "Roxanne" and the subsequent "Can't Stand Losing You," both of which were major hits.

The rest of his albums with the Police, from "Regatta De Blanc" onwards, were mostly recorded with fretless basses of various kinds, including an Ibanez Musician. Sting, showing a pioneering spirit, tried the Steinberger headless when it arrived in the early 1980s and ended his Police days with a Spector. An early bass in his solo career, which began in 1985, was a Fender Jazz.

In the 1990s he went back to the instrument and settled on a 1950s Precision bass with a vintage-style single-coil pickup, maple neck, and two-color sunburst finish. Unlike the earliest slab-bodied examples from 1951, this had a contoured "belly cut" at the top, but the Precision had not yet taken on the streamlined shape of the Stratocaster—it would do this in 1957. Sting has two of these; the first, believed to be a 1955 example, was purchased in New York in 1993 during the shooting of the Sylvester Stallone movie *Demolition Man* and was used on the soundtrack. (Legend has it he sent his roadie to buy the "oldest, most beat-up" bass he could find.) The second is a 1957 model, made that April, just before the body shape changed.

Both of Sting's basses are equipped with Seymour Duncan stacked single-coil Basslines pickups, which eliminate the annoying hum associated with all single-coil pickups while retaining the sound.

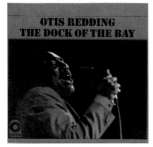

FENDER PRECISION BASS
DONALD "DUCK" DUNN

When Donald "Duck" Dunn replaced Lewis Steinberg as bass player of Booker T. and the MGs (Memphis Group) in 1965, he joined an outfit whose backing of Southern soul stars—like Wilson Pickett, Otis Redding, Sam and Dave, and Carla and Rufus Thomas—helped create the Stax label's enduring musical legacy.

Along with Booker T. Jones (organ, piano), Steve Cropper (guitar) and Al Jackson Jr. (drums), Dunn also played a part in creating tunes like "Hip Hug-Her," "Hang 'Em High," and "Soul Limbo" to add to the MGs' run of instrumental hits that started back in 1962. The racially integrated MGs were more than just a house band. But, while touring Britain in the Stax Revue of 1967, he went unrecognized. "Without being racist," he said, "they probably thought that, being affiliated with that music, Donald "Duck" Dunn was black!"

Among the timeless recordings on which Dunn and his Fender Precision featured are "Respect," "Dock of the Bay," and "I've Been Loving You Too Long," by Otis Redding; "In the Midnight Hour" by Wilson Pickett; and "Hold On I'm Coming" by Sam and Dave.

Dunn stepped into the spotlight as one of the Blues Brothers Band when that morphed out of *Saturday Night Live* in 1980. He's also graced the live bands of Eric Clapton and Neil Young. His instrument of choice is a candy-apple red late-1950s Fender Precision bass with a narrow Jazz-style neck. A replica of this was granted signature status by Fender and, later, Lakland.

Dunn is now semi-retired, having battled ill health in recent years, but is still revered as an economical player who knows the "right" notes. Dunn was also keen to improvise: "Even though we were playing the same songs every night I like to think I can change it a little bit and use my input or creativity or whatever in any way that makes the band feel better. If I make the band smile, I make everybody smile."

Notable Fender Precision bass players:
Motown's James Jamerson, who was very much Dunn's contemporary; Bob Babbitt (Motown); Geezer Butler (Black Sabbath); John Deacon (Queen); Roger Waters (Pink Floyd); Mike Dirnt (Green Day); Steve Harris (Iron Maiden); Nate Mendel (Foo Fighters); Jean Jacques Durnel (the Stranglers); Pete Wentz (Fall Out Boy); Colin Greenwood (Radiohead); Stu Cook (Creedence Clearwater Revival).

FENDER STRATOCASTER

STRAT OR SUPERSTRAT?

The Fender Stratocaster—or Strat, as it is universally abbreviated—has stood the test of time since its introduction in 1954. Designed by Leo Fender, George Fullerton, and Freddie Tavares, the Stratocaster made its appearance two years after the more expensive Les Paul, but soon made up for lost time. Its contoured body was slimmer than its rival, while its neck was bolted onto the body like all other Fenders, whereas the Les Paul's was more expensively glued, or "set."

It is by far the most popular shape of the past half-century, whether a Fender-made guitar or one of many copies. "Strat" has become a generic term, while "Superstrat" denotes a guitar with at least one humbucking pickup alongside one or two single coils.

As with its stablemate, the Telecaster, it was available only with a one-piece maple neck until 1959, when a glued rosewood fingerboard was offered as standard. In 1967 the maple option was reintroduced but glued onto the maple neck in order to install the stiffening truss rod without having to rout out the back of the neck. The one-piece maple neck made a comeback in 1970. Many players consider the 1959–65 Strats, with their slimmer necks, to have the best and most comfortable neck profiles.

THE TREMOLO

The Strat's vibrato unit, commonly known as tremolo or whammy bar, was a big part of its success and was something neither its rival Les Paul nor the Telecaster had. Leo Fender and Freddie Tavares scrapped their original design but came up with a winner the second time around. The bridge and tailpiece formed one unit, which pivoted at the front and was balanced against string tension by five adjustable springs underneath the body. It also had six separate string saddles, allowing individual height and intonation to be achieved.

The Strat changed little over the years, though the headstock became larger in 1965 to match the Jazzmaster and Jaguar and to help combat neck-warping problems that had been encountered. In practice, many "vintage" Strat reissues have been marketed, allowing today's players to own and play a guitar associated with a golden era of music and guitar

playing. The takeover of Fender by CBS in 1965 led to a perceived drop in quality control, and pre-CBS Strats have always commanded premium prices.

PICKUPS

The Fender Stratocaster rivals Gibson's Les Paul as the most iconic guitar in rock. It is certainly the most imitated by other makers (Charvel, Burns, Schecter, and others), the tonal variation available from its three single-coil pickups being unparalleled. A Superstrat configuration has also evolved with a humbucker replacing one of the single coils to fatten the sound. A three-way pickup selection switch could be wedged between settings to obtain an out-of-phase sound.

A distinctive chrome jack socket gave a diagonal entry to the body and meant there would be less damage if a lead pulled out accidentally. The headstock size of Strats is probably the most obvious distinguishing feature between marks and models, but all shared the same basic features.

SUNBURST FINISH

In its original form, the Stratocaster was offered initially in a two-color sunburst finish with a solid, deeply contoured ash body, a one-piece maple neck with twenty-one frets, black dot inlays, and Kluson machine heads. In 1957 Fender started producing bodies made from solid alder. Custom colors were available, mostly automobile lacquer colors made by Dupont, and could be applied for an extra 5 percent of the guitar price. The single-ply eight-screw-hole white pickguard was a unique concept that allowed all of the guitar's electronic components—except the recessed jack plate—to be (cost-effectively) mounted on one easy-to-remove surface.

Subsequent Stratocaster designs by both Fender and other imitating companies have supposedly improved upon the original in usability and sound; but vintage Fenders are still often worth large amounts of money, and many guitarists prefer older models.

The main image at left is a Stratocaster from 1954. Above, in descending order are a red 1961 Strat, a blue 1969 Strat, a wine red 1980 Strat, and a 40th Anniversary Stratocaster, produced in 1994.

FENDER STRATOCASTER
ERIC CLAPTON

Ever since he burst onto the scene with the Yardbirds in 1963, guitarists have been watching how Eric Clapton plays and what he plays. He brought the Les Paul back into fashion through his work with John Mayall's Bluesbreakers, but it was the inspiration of Jimi Hendrix that turned him on to the Fender Stratocaster, his guitar of choice since the early seventies.

Best known of these is Blackie, a hybrid guitar he assembled himself from a 1956 alder body, finished in black nitrocellulose lacquer with a maple neck, which would enjoy twelve years and thirteen solo albums in the spotlight between 1973 and 1985. Clapton's second solo album, *461 Ocean Boulevard*, had Blackie's signature all over it, not least on his version of Bob Marley's "I Shot The Sheriff," which established his solo status in 1974 by topping the U.S. singles chart.

An accidental fall during a session for *461* in Jamaica made Clapton realize how important the guitar had become to him in such a short time. He crushed the body and neck in the accident but, after a few running repairs, it was playing as good as new. "That's when I thought: this guitar is my life, I can pick it up, drop it or bounce it off the wall and it will still be in tune and play with heart and soul. It's irreplaceable."

Blackie appears on the cover of 1977's *Slowhand*. Hits from that album include "Wonderful Tonight," "Lay Down Sally," and "Cocaine"—three tracks that alone ensure the instrument

a place in rock history. It took its final live bow at Live Aid in 1985 and, in 2004, became the most valuable guitar ever to be sold at auction when it made $959,500 for the Crossroads Centre, the drug and alcohol rehabilitation center Clapton founded in Antigua.

FENDER STRATOCASTER
DAVID GILMOUR

David Gilmour joined Pink Floyd at the beginning of 1968 as an additional guitarist when frontman Syd Barrett's increasingly unstable behavior was becoming a liability. The idea proved impractical and Barrett left, leaving Gilmour to become an influential presence alongside bassist and founding member Roger Waters.

The pair fell out during the making of 1979's *The Wall*, and after one further album Gilmour assumed the mantle of bandleader, reinstating kicked-out keyboardist Richard Wright.

Gilmour's chosen guitar has always been a Stratocaster, and he was present when Fender celebrated its golden anniversary at Wembley Arena, London, in 2004. He brought with him an early white Strat (serial number 001), which is not actually the first but is believed to date from 1954, the first year of production.

His trademark Strat, however, is a 1969-made black model (overpainted on a sunburst finish) with a maple neck and standard Fender tremolo, which featured on numerous Floyd albums such as *Dark Side of the Moon*, *Wish You Were Here*, and *The Wall*. It has also played a major role in Gilmour's solo projects including, notably, his 2006 U.K. Number 1 album, *On an Island*. The track "Comfortably Numb," from *The Wall*, has been singled out as its finest few minutes, as have the first two or three guitar solos in "Money" from *Dark Side of the Moon*.

"It was just an ordinary Strat that I bought at [New York guitar shop] Manny's," said Gilmour, who purchased it in 1970. The first one he bought got stolen on the same U.S. tour, and Gilmour made a trip back to Manny's on the group's way home to London and bought what is now his legendary Black Stratocaster.

It has been constantly modified; its neck was replaced in 1972, while a humbucking

pickup was added in the central position in 1973. In September 2008 Fender confirmed they would release a signature model, while guitar technician Phil Taylor has written a copiously illustrated book on it, *The Black Strat*. The guitar acquired a black pickguard in summer 1974, hence its nickname.

Notable Stratocaster players: Jimi Hendrix; Jeff Beck; Steve Miller; Jeff Healey; Robin Trower; Eddie Clarke (Motörhead); Hank Marvin; Mark Knopfler; Stevie Ray Vaughan.

FENDER TELECASTER

THE BROADCASTER

The Fender Telecaster was the brainchild of Clarence Leonidas "Leo" Fender, a man who famously could not play a single chord on the guitar. But there is no doubt that he knew what musicians wanted. In 1948 he introduced a solid-body prototype, the Broadcaster; it remains an industry standard today and, along with the Stratocaster and Precision bass, a jewel in Fender's crown. Its name was changed to Telecaster two years later, as the Gretsch company was using "Broadkaster," with a "k," on a drum kit. Retailing at a price of $189.50, the Tele would become a staple of the country musician's armory before spreading to pop and rock. With no hollow body to contend with, the problem of feedback was almost nonexistent. Advertising copy extolled the virtue of a "thinner body, which makes playing for long periods less tiring." The guitar was basic but fit its purpose, and it tended to be adopted by players in fields where sound, not image, was paramount.

TELECASTER CUSTOM

In the 1970s, the introduction of a humbucking pickup at the neck resulted in the Telecaster Custom. This gave an option of adding a rock "oomph" to the sound, similar to modifications made by Keith Richards, Andy Summers, and others. The model boasted different and more numerous rotary controls, while the Tele's trademark sliding-pickup selector was replaced by a Gibson-style selector switch. Indeed, purists thought this a Gibson in Fender clothing.

BOLT-ON NECK

The solid-bodied Fender Telecaster was a basic instrument, but one that delivered. Prototypes in the then-standard blond finish that were taken to music-instrument shows were derided as "canoe paddles" or "snow shovels" due to their uncontoured bodies, but Leo Fender had the last laugh.

The Tele's maple neck was unceremoniously attached to the body with four retaining bolts and a

plate, banjo-style, rather than being glued in Gibson-style. Metal frets were sunk directly into the maple neck rather than having a separate rosewood fingerboard glued on before fret application. Some early Esquires (as the first Teles were known) were returned to the manufacturer with warped necks, so including a truss rod to keep the neck straight was a necessary modification.

GUITAR OF THE PEOPLE

The Telecaster was always intended as a mass-produced instrument. Its slab body was band sawed from slabs of wood, unlike the elaborately carved bodies of Gibson guitars. The bridge and tailpiece, separate components on most guitars, were combined in a simple pressed-steel unit, while the elongated control plate housing pickup selector and volume and tone controls was removable for easy access to internal wiring. These simplifications could be and were reflected in the price of less than $200, but players reveled in the simplicity and durability of what would become the Ford Model T of electric guitars. It has never gone out of production or fashion—and there seems no likelihood it ever will. All you need to do with a good Tele is tune it.

The main image below is a Fender Telecaster from 1952. Above, in descending order are a red 1959 Telecaster, a buff 1966 Telecaster with Bigsby tremolo arm, a 1967 sunburst Telecaster Custom, a 1971 Telecaster Thinline (with a hollow cavity on its bass side and f-hole), and finally a paisley-colored Tele displaying the bolt-on plate.

FENDER TELECASTER
KEITH RICHARDS

The human riff on which the Rolling Stones have relied since 1962 has been associated with many guitars. But "Micawber," a blonde 1953 Fender Telecaster named after a Charles Dickens character, is probably one of Keith Richards's most famous guitars. "There's no reason for my guitar being called Micawber," he said in 1992, "apart from the fact that it's such an unlikely name. There's no one around me called Micawber, so when I scream for Micawber everybody knows what I'm talking about." Richards has played this guitar since the early 1970s and *Exile on Main St.* This guitar is kept in open G tuning (G–D–G–B–D), low to high with no capo. It has the sixth string removed, as do all his open G-tuned guitars. "The thing about the five string tuning," he says, "is that you need five strings, you get three notes, you use two fingers, and you get one ****hole to play it! But to me it rejuvenated my enthusiasm for playing guitar, because you'd put your fingers where you thought they'd go and you'd get accidents happening, and you wouldn't've done on regular tuning, because you'd know it too well.... You just turn a few pegs and get a different tuning and suddenly you get, almost like, a different instrument. It gave me a lot of renewed interest in playing the guitar."

Micawber has replacement tuners and a brass replacement bridge with individual saddles, and the nut is cut to accommodate five strings (they aren't evenly spaced across the fingerboard, but the first string is moved in a little to keep it from going over the edge). It has a Gibson PAF ("Patent Applied For") humbucker in the neck position and an original Tele pickup in the bridge position. Its characteristic warm sound can be heard on such live tracks as "Before They Make Me Run," "Brown Sugar," "Mixed Emotions," and "Honky Tonk Women." A trim ring around the humbucker is there because the hole in the original pickguard was cut too large for the new pickup. This is believed to have been installed upside down, intentionally or not. Richards's other main stage Telecasters are "Malcolm," a 1954 example in natural finish, and "Sonny," a sunburst from 1966. Both are also kept in open G tuning.

FENDER TELECASTER
BRUCE SPRINGSTEEN

When Bruce Springsteen emerged from New Jersey in the early seventies, his blue-collar-hero persona needed a guitar that was as unostentatious as himself, a musical tool as down-to-earth as a flatbed truck. He found it in the Telecaster, and has never deviated from his choice in thirty-five years at the top.

Springsteen plays both lead and rhythm on his Telecaster, which started life in 1953/54 as a single-pickup Esquire before having a second pickup added. It was modified with a battery-operated impedance transformer to cope with long cable lengths, which was an unavoidable problem before the introduction of wireless systems.

Unknown to all but the fanatical, there is an asterisk in front of the Esquire's serial number, indicating that it was a factory reject and was probably sold as such. This "reject" has graced "Born to Run" (including the iconic ascending run with a saxophone), "The River," "Born in the USA," and countless other hits. Indeed, the *Born to Run* album cover sees him with his Telecaster in typical stage pose.

In an interview for the album's thirtieth anniversary, he claimed the guitar is a hybrid of two guitars, a Telecaster body and Esquire neck. It is more accurately described as a first-generation Esquire. These had two pickup routs, as the pickguard covered the neck hole, but his has had a neck pickup installed.

Though fellow E Street Band guitarists Steve Van Zandt and Nils Lofgren favor the Stratocaster, Springsteen takes his share of the leads, but eschews effects. "I have a very fundamental setup on the guitar. There's a loud button and a louder one and a louder one than that—and that's it!"

There has been no signature Bruce Springsteen Telecaster model to date, much to

Fender's chagrin, the reason being that Springsteen doesn't want his name to be used in a commercial context. Nor does the signature concept fit the Tele, which now, as in the beginning, is everyman's guitar.

Notable Telecaster players: Users have ranged from punk Joe Strummer to blues-man Albert "Iceman" Collins. Others include Sheryl Crow; Steve Cropper (Booker T and the MGs); Wilko Johnson (Dr. Feelgood); Jonny Buckland (Coldplay); Frank Black; Denny Dias (Steely Dan); Mike Campbell (Tom Petty and the Heartbreakers); Graham Coxon (Blur); Rick Parfitt and Francis Rossi (Status Quo); Bob Dylan (post-Newport).

GIBSON EB-3
JACK BRUCE

Scottish rock icon Jack Bruce emerged from a jazz background to change the face of rock music as one third of Cream. The concept of three instrumental virtuosi soloing through each song was groundbreaking, and his work with Eric Clapton and Ginger Baker from 1966 to 1968 made him one of the highest-profile rock musicians of the era. He was inspired to become a bass player when his father took him to the Jazz at the Phil tour in the 1950s and he saw the great American double bassist Ray Brown.

Though trained on the upright bass, Bruce moved on to small, short-scale electric basses. One of his first was the Fender Bass VI, a six-string bass tuned like a guitar but one octave lower, with which he recorded most of *Fresh Cream* before moving to the short-scale four-string Gibson EB-3. "I wanted to develop a style of playing that was very guitarlike, instead of playing root notes. I used La Bella light-gauge strings, which I could bend."

Bruce sometimes plugged this into a 100-watt Marshall guitar

GIBSON EB-3

Gibson's EB (Electric Bass) series was launched in 1953 with a short-scale solid-body bass that looked like a miniature double bass with painted-on f-hole. This was retrospectively named EB-1 after the launch in 1958 of the semi-acoustic EB-2, the four-string counterpart of the ES-335 guitar. A third design, the EB-3, then appeared in 1961 to complement the identically bodied SG guitar.

It was most commonly seen as a short-scale (30.5-inch) instrument, though an EB-3L was offered at the start of the 1970s, and had pickups at the neck and bridge. The similar EB-0 was a single-pickup variant, introduced at the same time, and both shared the rosewood fingerboard and unfussy two-a-side headstock that was again reminiscent of the six-string SG. The standard finish was cherry red, though EB-3s were less often produced in finishes such as Polaris White, Pelham Blue, and Ebony.

Costs were saved by the combination of bridge and tailpiece into a weighty dual-function piece of nickel-plated hardware based on the Tune-o-matic guitar bridge. A four-way Varitone rotary control with

"chicken-head" knob offered different tonal variations.

The Gibson Sidewinder humbucker at the neck was massive in both size and sound, while the Gibson minihumbucker at the bridge sounded somewhat anemic on its own. Using the minihumbucker in combination with the Sidewinder added some much-needed guts.

The design of this bass, as with its guitar relative, has been criticized for the tendency of the neck to "dive" toward the ground because of the small body and large headstock. A slotted headstock was introduced on later examples but had little effect.

Ultimately, Gibson failed to break through as a bass manufacturer despite the introduction of the sexier, long-scale Thunderbird. The Gibson EB-3 was discontinued in the late 1970s but is currently being produced by Epiphone in both long-scale and short-scale versions.

Despite having two pickups and a four-way Varitone control (the larger circular knob), the Gibson EB-3, modeled on the SG guitar, had little variation in usable sounds.

stack. The thick, distorted sound he obtained helped fill out the sound of an instrumental three-piece. And while the Gibson EB series of basses never rivaled Fender's domination of the bottom-end market, Bruce's patronage gave them more of a foothold than they might otherwise have enjoyed.

"I wanted to play bass like a guitar, and you can't do that on a regular Fender; you can't bend the strings. And since I was the lead vocalist, I needed some kind of compact instrument that I could more or less forget about while I was singing. But probably the most important reason was that I didn't want it to sound like a Fender!" He was assisted by pickup guru Dan Armstrong, who installed a diode in the guitar to increase distortion.

Bruce used the EB-3 all the way from Cream's *Disraeli Gears* through solo albums like *Songs for a Tailor* and *Harmony Row*, and with 1970s power trio West, Bruce, and Laing.

Notable Gibson EB-3 players: Andy Fraser (Free); Trevor Bolder (formerly a Spider from Mars); Mike Watt (the Stooges); Phil Lesh (the Grateful Dead).

GIBSON EDS-1275
DON FELDER

The Eagles defined the sound of California in the 1970s and were its most successful exponents. Don Felder joined for third album *On the Border* (1974), for which the Eagles switched studios to Los Angeles and to producer Bill Szymczyk.

It was Felder who came up with the signature riff for the title track of *Hotel California* (1976), the Eagles' masterwork. It was recorded in the studio on a Martin twelve-string acoustic with a pickup that was run through a Leslie (rotating speaker) cabinet and recorded in stereo. But he used one of two

Gibson EDS-1275 double-neck guitars to play the song live until he parted company with the Eagles in 2001. (Led Zeppelin's Jimmy Page similarly used his to play both the verse and solo sections of "Stairway to Heaven" onstage without having to change guitars.)

Felder drilled another hole in it to add a second output jack. "Then I rewired it so that one neck goes out one output and the other goes out the second. The output changes with the neck selector switch. I ran the twelve-string neck into a echo unit and a Leslie and the six-string neck into my pedalboard and then into a Fender Deluxe amp."

After an acrimonious split, the Eagles reunited in 1994 for the Hell Freezes Over tour. The resulting CD included an acoustic Latin version of "Hotel California." And while the introduction was reworked to be more Spanish and acoustic, it was again the silhouette of Felder and his double neck that was the first thing audiences saw.

Notable Gibson EDS-1275 players:
Jimmy Page (Led Zeppelin); Alex Lifeson (Rush); Steve Clark (Def Leppard); John McLaughlin (the Mahavishnu Orchestra).

GIBSON EDS-1275

The Gibson double-neck guitar is a derivative of the Gibson SG, though original models, produced between 1958 and 1962, were twin hollow-body instruments with dual cutaways similar to the ES-175. The addition of the letter "D" and the number "2" indicated the twin necks.

These early models are quite rare. The newer, more common version was available in cherry red, ebony, and arctic white.

The guitar body is made of solid mahogany and features two volume and two tone controls: a selector switch activates each guitar, while a three-way selector switch allows a choice between pickups. The necks are each of three-piece maple construction, bound with single-ply white binding and topped with rosewood fingerboards. The neck scale length is 24.75 inches. Other features include vintage tulip-shaped tuners and pearloid split-parallelogram fretboard inlays.

Gibson stopped production of the EDS-1275 in 1968 and reintroduced the model again in 1977. The EDS-1275 is now no longer a regular production model and is only available in cherry or alpine white through the Gibson Custom Shop.

The EDS-1275 in Jimmy Page's favored cherry red (below). Note the six-string's pickups have exposed covers, in contrast to their twelve-string counterparts.

GIBSON ES-175
IZZY STRADLIN

While Slash supplied the style of late-1980s trash-rock icons Guns N' Roses, the role of guitar partner Jeff Isbell, better known as Izzy Stradlin, shouldn't be underestimated.

Slash fulfilled the Keef role to Axl Rose's Jaggeresque preening—yet Stradlin's rhythm-guitar style owed far more to Mr Richards than his companion's Les Paul leads. He was also Axl's main songwriting partner.

His use of a Gibson ES-175 semi-acoustic through Mesa/Boogie amps gave him a sound that was, in his words, "a growling sound, kind of twangy." It certainly provided an effective contrast to Slash's Les Paul/Marshall combination. "Before Izzy," Slash revealed, "I'd never been able to play with another guitarist."

Stradlin was quick to return the compliment. "We both really loved Aerosmith and the Stones and we just used that idea to make it all work." The duo's understanding became so telepathic that they even switched lead and rhythm roles on occasion: for instance, Stradlin plays solo on "Think About You" and the first half of the (pre-chorus) solo on "Nightrain."

Stradlin's contributions to *Appetite for Destruction* and *Use Your Illusion*, were mostly on his Gibson ES-175, which remained his standard stage guitar. Stradlin said:

"I like Les Pauls, but the hollowbodies are great, because I can play them in hotel rooms or anywhere without an amp. I just love the look, the feel, and the sound those things get. Especially those old soapbar pickups—I've yet to find anything that can match that. I have a couple of Gibson Byrdlands with the Florentine cutaway, a half-dozen Les Pauls, a couple triple-pickup Les Paul Customs, a couple of 1970s Telecasters, a couple of 335s and a few ES-175s. I play through old Fender Bassman heads with a Mesa Boogie 4x12 cabinet with EV speakers in the bottom. It gets a real thick, warm sound. My preference is EVs on the bottom and Celestions on top. The Bassmans are the 1960s blackface models, and I run everything on around five."

Notable ES-175 players: Steve Howe (Yes); George Thorogood.

GIBSON ES-175

When former Wurlitzer organ supremo Ted McCarty became Gibson president in 1950 he quickly moved them into the electric guitar field as serious challengers to Fender.

The single-cutaway ES-175 semi-acoustic was the immediate predecessor to the Les Paul and was at that time top of the ES (Electric Spanish) range. If the Les Paul's impact on the world of rock and blues was titanic, the ES-175 had the same effect in the realm of jazz. It was designed as an electric guitar—not as an acoustic with a pickup—and has enjoyed the longest continuous production run of any electric guitar.

When the Gibson ES-175 debuted in 1949, it nudged aside the ES-150, which had been the guitar of choice for jazz innovators like Charlie Christian and Eddie Durham. The ES-175 also proved a more manageable and less costly ($175) alternative to the L-5, thanks to its smaller body size and laminated top. It

was also the first Gibson electric to feature a Florentine cutaway.

Its first incarnation had one single-coil pickup (a P-90) in the neck position, and a carved rosewood bridge. In 1953, the ES-175D, a two-pickup model, was introduced. The ES-175 or ES-175D could be ordered in either sunburst or natural finish. The guitar's appellation came from the price tag of the first ES: $175.

The 175 lacks the booming acoustic power of its two bigger brothers, the Super 400 and the ES-5, but what is lost in volume is gained in playability: it's the easiest to play thanks to its size, low action, and fast neck that is accessible to the fourteenth fret. The 175 delivers a sweet, clean, amplified tone.

The sedate appearance of the ES-175, a guitar intended for jazz noodling, can be deceptive, given that it has provided the backbone to many Guns N' Roses hits.

GIBSON ES-295
SCOTTY MOORE

Elvis Presley, a poor man's son from Tupelo, Mississippi, brought together the threads of white country and black blues to create what we now know as rock 'n' roll. And when Elvis walked into Sun Studio in Memphis, Tennessee, in July 1954 to cut his first single, guitarist Winfield Scott "Scotty" Moore was by his side. Moore's rockabilly licks, played on a semi-acoustic Gibson ES-295, added instrumental excitement to the likes of "That's All Right," "Good Rockin' Tonight," and "Mystery Train."

Moore had bought an Esquire (Telecaster) in 1952 but switched to a new Gibson ES-295 in 1953. He used the 295 on tour and all but the last Sun recordings with Elvis, trading it in 1955 for a Gibson L5 and thence a blonde Gibson Super 400. The latter was heard on "Jailhouse Rock," "King Creole," and Elvis's first post-Army sessions.

Moore says he made the transition from the ES 295 to the L5 in time for the Sun session that produced "Mystery Train." "I never used a solid guitar, and I've never used small gauge strings—I just bled a lot!" Brian Setzer of the Stray Cats has referred to the ES-295 as "the ultimate rockabilly guitar," though Moore believes the L5 "was probably the better guitar for our kind of music."

Even though Moore only played an ES-295 during the early months of his recording career, the musical history he helped make with it has ensured he became synonymous with the instrument. He replaced the stock trapeze tailpiece with a more traditional tailpiece and a Melita bridge—as used on many mid-1950s Gretsch guitars—to allow for more accurate intonation. The amplifier it went through was built by Ray Butts. Moore obtained one of his EchoSonic amps after hearing Chet Atkins using one. "Boy, I can tell you that when I first plugged in and turned that thing on I said, 'That's it!'" Moore still has the amplifier and it is still in working condition.

The ES-295 guitar, used by one of the most influential rock guitarists of all time on those historic Elvis recordings, was bought by Jimmy Velvet, a longtime friend of Presley, for $6,000. It was sold in the early 1990s for $125,000.

GIBSON ES-295

Gibson produced the ES-295 from 1952 to 1959. They reintroduced them in 1994 but then again discontinued them. The model was based on the ES-175 and shared its single-cutaway body, bound maple top, f-holes, and raised white pickguard with etched flowers. A bronze metallic finish was a distinguishing feature. Gibson only built 1,770 of this model on the original run, so today a 1950s ES-295 in any condition is rare indeed.

The guitar had a maple back and sides with a mahogany neck, a nineteen-fret bound rosewood fingerboard decorated by pearl parallelogram inlays, and a black-painted wood-veneer peg head with crown logo inlay.

On the body, it had a trapeze wrap-over tailpiece, which Moore replaced, gold hardware, and two white single-coil P-90 pickups. PAF humbuckers replaced these for the last few produced in 1958. Two volume and tone controls governed these, a standard three-way switch on the upper bout facilitating selection.

Around 2007 Moore was reunited with his original ES-295, now owned by a Memphis collector, to talk about it for a video. It was the first time he'd played it since 1955.

GIBSON ES-325
CALEB FOLLOWILL

When Nathan and Caleb Followill were struggling Nashville-based youngsters intent on launching Kings of Leon, they were fortunate to fall in with songwriter/producer Angelo Petraglia. The introduction had come through his music publishing company, and Petraglia was key in shaping the early Kings of Leon sound. He also placed a bevy of classic rock guitars in their hands, allowing access to his vast collection of vintage Gibsons and Epiphones.

Early in the songwriting process he handed Caleb his precious 1972 Gibson ES-325. He'd bought the semi-acoustic rarity on the Internet auction site eBay for a bargain $900. That precious 325 would appear on all the band's subsequent records and was also played on stage until it met a violent death at 2009's T in the Park Festival in Scotland.

GIBSON ES-325

Gibson's ES (Electro Spanish) series of semi-acoustic guitars became relatively less important to the company's profitability after their solid-body Les Paul took off in the early 1950s, but they certainly had no intention of discontinuing their work in the jazz field where these guitars had become ubiquitous. The ES-325 was, however, less widely seen than most.

While similar in appearance to the more popular ES-335, this was a different guitar in both construction and sound. While the ES-335 was a semihollow guitar (the central part of the guitar body was a solid block while the wings of the guitar were hollow), the Thinline 325 had just one f-hole and a plastic control plate that housed the volume and tone control knobs. This correctly gave the appearance of a cheaper alternative to its opulent big brother.

The ES-325 featured two minihumbucking pickups with non-adjustable pole pieces, similar to those used on the Gibson Firebird. The guitar was available in walnut and cherry finishes, while both trapeze and stop-tail tailpieces were available. The neck was topped with a twenty-two-fret rosewood fingerboard with unobtrusive dot inlays.

Due to its lack of popularity compared to the other Gibson semi-acoustic guitars, Gibson discontinued the ES-325 in the late 1970s.

Volume and tone controls mounted on a separate semicircular scratchplate immediately mark out the ES-325 from its more-often-seen brothers in the Gibson semi-acoustic range.

Sound problems proved the final straw and the performance almost ended in blows between band members. Caleb had taken his frustration out on his beloved Gibson, smashing it as the set finished and casting its broken remains into the crowd. A source at the festival told the press: "He was livid about the sound and took out his anger on stage without considering the consequences."

The guitar would certainly be a big loss. In the words of one magazine, it was "a stunning workhorse instrument that bears the unmistakable marks of the singer-guitarist's ferocious, percussive style of strumming." Guitar technician "Nacho" had previously commented that if anything happened to that guitar, he'd "just pack up and head home, it was that special."

Speaking to the *Scottish Daily Record* newspaper after the gig, Caleb explained his actions: "I got a bit angry and broke my guitar, so I have to get a new one. We have zero reasons to complain, but I do blame me breaking my guitar on being overworked. I would never, ever dream of doing anything to that guitar. It's moments like that where you realize you need a break."

It was never going to be as popular as its big brother the ES-335, and while Eric Clapton is rumored to have used one briefly in the past, Caleb Followill is the only player whose signature instrument it is today.

GIBSON ES-335/345 "LUCILLE"
B. B. KING

Brought up in Mississippi, Riley B. King went on to become one of the blues' most influential guitarists—his albums were being nominated for Grammies half a century after his recording debut. He was inspired by hearing T-Bone Walker in the late 1930s. "From that time on," he said, "I knew what I wanted to do: I did anything anybody asked just to make enough money to buy me a guitar."

An inability to sing and play at the same time saw him adopt a call-and-response routine with his guitar, the to-and-fro effect echoing gospel. Another "limitation," a lack of facility at slide playing, led to his developing another musical trademark—a unique mix of vibrato and sustain, which, combined with almost constantly bending notes on a single string, resulted in a guitar sound that was very much his own. He has never used a vibrato tailpiece, believing "the reason people came out with that was because they were trying to duplicate the sound I was getting with my left hand....I don't need it!"

The first "Lucille," the name he gave his semi-acoustic Gibson, arrived in 1958; prior to that he'd used Fender, Gretsch, and Epiphone guitars. "I even had a Silvertone from Sears

Roebuck," he says of the ubiquitous "catalog" guitar. "But when I found that little Gibson with the long neck that did it. That's like finding your wife forever." King preferred the 345 variant, wired for stereo, because he believed it accentuated the highs: "I can't hear the lows, my ears don't tell me too much, but highs I can hear very well."

Lucille has "taken me a long way, even brought me some fame.... Most of all, she's kept me alive, being able to eat. Lucille practically saved my life two or three times," he says, referring to one of his several auto accidents. "The car stopped turning over, it fell over on Lucille and it held it up off of me."

Notable Gibson ES-335/ES-345 players:
Andrew White (Kaiser Chiefs); Bill Nelson.

GIBSON 335/345 "LUCILLE"

Having found success with the solid-bodied Les Paul series, Gibson returned to hollow-bodied jazz guitars in 1958 with the intention of creating a hybrid. The result was the ES-335—the ES standing for Electro Spanish. This had a solid block of maple running through the center of the body on which bridge, tailpiece, and pickup were all mounted, offering solid-body sustain while the rest of the body could amplify and add depth to the sound.

Two violin-style f-holes were positioned over the side-wing sound chambers, the idea being to offer a warmer tone than the Les Paul but minimizing the feedback associated with acoustic designs. It also debuted a new bridge, dubbed the Tune-o-matic (later applied to the Les Paul), and had a slim, comfortable neck.

Variations included the ES-345, which had a Varitone switch, a parametric equalizer with five presets, and was wired for stereo with two output jacks. The headstock of the 355 had a split-diamond inlay rather than the smaller inlay on the 335. The fingerboard inlays are blocks, inlaid on the fretboard, rather than the original dots. Binding was applied to the headstock, the fretboard, and both the front and the back of the body.

Gibson made the Lucille the first signature model accorded by a black musician when they made it available in 1980. The Custom was based on the ES-345TD-SV with stereo wiring and Varitone circuitry. The wood used to make the neck was maple instead of mahogany for a brighter sound. The split-diamond headstock inlay on the ES-355 was replaced by the word "Lucille" in script. Last but not least, the Lucille had no f-holes on its top.

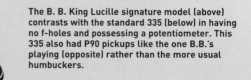

The B. B. King Lucille signature model (above) contrasts with the standard 335 (below) in having no f-holes and possessing a potentiometer. This 335 also had P90 pickups like the one B.B.'s playing (opposite) rather than the more usual humbuckers.

GIBSON EXPLORER
THE EDGE

Though he's rung the changes over the years, U2's lead guitarist, Dave Evans—The Edge—used a Gibson Explorer played through a 50-watt Marshall combo almost exclusively in the band's early Dublin days. He bought the guitar at age seventeen while in New York with his parents. "It was just so naturally good, and it felt right, so I bought it....A lot of people look at it and think it's one of the originals but it's one of the 1976 limited-edition reissue models."

When U2 formed he wondered what reception the angular guitar would get, but it became a signature look of the band. The Edge feels it's also the most tonally distinctive of his guitars and believes the body shape affects the sound. "It's a very vibrant guitar with lots of treble."

Indeed, it was a significant influence on how he developed his style of playing. "The bass end of the Explorer was so awful that I used to stay away from the low strings, and a lot of the chords I played on the first four, or even three strings were very trebly. Through using this one area of the fretboard I was developing a very stylized way of doing something that someone else would play in a normal way."

He used it for the first album, *Boy* (1980), and up until the recording of

GIBSON EXPLORER

Gibson's final creations of the 1950s, the Explorer and Flying V, were futuristic designs that would only be fully embraced by players in years to come. Its twin humbucking pickups offered similar tonal possibilities to the Les Paul and SG, which conservative guitarists preferred.

The Explorer was the final development of a prototype design which, years later, Gibson marketed under the name Futura. But its shape made it ideal for pretty-boy posing, and many other manufacturers have used it as the basis for their own heavy-metal-directed designs—for example, Hamer, Dean, Robin, Aria, Washburn, Ibanez, and BC Rich.

With its angular, asymmetrical body and pointed headstock, the Explorer was such a radical departure that Gibson produced only about 100 of the original korina-wood-bodied model. These are now highly collectible and sell for upwards of half a million dollars. Explorers made between 1957 and 1958 are identifiable by an unusual split-shaped head with the tuners placed in a standard "three plus three" arrangement.

The Explorer was reintroduced in the mid-1970s after other companies' copies had emphasized the demand. Variants included smaller-bodied versions such as the X-Plorer Studio, the Explorer 90 (designed by Matthias Jabs of the Scorpions and 90 percent the body size of a regular Explorer), and the Explorer Pro, introduced in 2007.

An Explorer with gold-plated hardware and a vibrato unit similar to the one available on the Flying V. The Edge prefers to add electronic effects to his music, playing a hard-tail instrument (opposite).

the follow-up, *October* (1981). It has remained a tried and trusted weapon in his guitar armory and has been used on selected later tracks, such as 2000's "Beautiful Day."

The Electro-Harmonix Memory Man echo unit combined with the Explorer, in Edge's words, "add seasoning to the soup....We became aware of different flavors in our music we hadn't known existed." One of his techniques that worked well with the Explorer was to make two strings ring the same note, emulating a twelve-string sound.

The Explorer survived a broken neck during a concert at New York's Radio City Music Hall in the mid-1980s after he threw the guitar off to intervene in a crowd melee. Luckily, the extensive repair didn't affect the sound.

Notable Explorer players: James Hetfield (Metallica); Brian Bell (Weezer); Dave Grohl (Foo Fighters); Dave Keuning (the Killers).

GIBSON FIREBIRD
PHIL MANZANERA

Roxy Music was one of the first groups of the 1970s to promote image as being as important as the music. Their guitarist, Phil Manzanera, had played a Gibson 335 with his previous band, Quiet Sun, but when he toured with Roxy Music he was told to change. "The vibe was I should have a white Strat, being the iconic guitar," he explained. This was, of course, in the wake of the recently deceased and already deified Jimi Hendrix."

The band's image developed and Manzanera

GIBSON FIREBIRD

Gibson's first new design of the 1960s, the Firebird, was introduced in 1963 and could have been designed with posing in mind. It was as if an Explorer had been given some extra streamlining. The lack of an upper horn made the body look almost aerodynamic in its flowing contours, with an extended lower horn, gaining it the nickname "reverse" or "reverse body."

This was the first Gibson to be built with a neck-through construction, meaning the body consisted of wooden "wings" added to either side of the extended neck. This was said to aid sustain. Fender complained that the design as it was originally produced mimicked their "offset waist" guitars like the Jaguar and Jazzmaster, so in 1965 Fender changed the body of later examples to a "nonreverse" shape. They also reverted to set (glued) necks, as featured by the Les Paul and SG.

The standard Gibson three-a-side tuning-peg layout has been discarded in favor of an upside-down Fender profile, with banjo-style tuners that could not be seen from the front at all.

Four models were offered, starting with the Firebird I, which had one pickup and no vibrato unit. The III doubled the pickups, while the V added a Tune-o-matic bridge to them. Finally the Firebird VII had three pickups and was the top of the line. The pickups used throughout were minihumbuckers.

The Firebird, like the Explorer, did not enjoy the success of Gibson's other models. It would prove an endangered species, and, despite Eric Clapton playing one in the Cream farewell concerts, by 1969 it and its Thunderbird bass counterpart had disappeared from the catalog. It would only be fully embraced by players in later decades.

The Firebird in its original and most impressive reverse-body shape. Phil Manzanera's unusual red instrument is believed to have been made in 1964.

found a red Gibson Firebird for sale in the classified ads of *Melody Maker*. So the white Strat appeared on the first eponymous Roxy Music album and the Firebird on the second, *For Your Pleasure*. Manzanera had never seen anyone else "except possibly Brian Jones" with a red Firebird. The previous owner had bought it from Gibson's Kalamazoo facility, from which it had emerged with a customized factory finish.

The Roxy Music track to which he feels the Firebird made the biggest contribution appeared on the third album, *Stranded*, and was titled "Amazona." The guitar was filtered by Brian Eno through a VCS3 synthesizer and then sent through a Revox tape recorder with long delays. "The amazing thing was that was probably the only time it actually worked, and at the end of that take everybody was clapping like mad as no one had heard anything like it before. It sounded like some underwater guitar."

The riff, "played on the red Firebird going through that whole system," was used as a theme on the TV show *Will & Grace*.

Notable Firebird players: Brian Jones; Johnny Winter; Eric Clapton; Gem Archer (Oasis).

GIBSON FLYING V
JIMI HENDRIX

While he was one of the world's most famous Stratocaster players, Jimi Hendrix put the Gibson Flying V on the map in September 1967. As he put the finishing touches to his second album, *Axis: Bold as Love*, he revealed another love of his guitar-playing life. The first photographic evidence connecting him with it came that September when he used it on stage in Sweden.

Hendrix was an Albert King fan, and one of the Flying V's attractions for left-handed players (which both men were) was that it offered unlimited access to the fretboard when

reversed from a right-handed orientation. King played it with right-handed stringing, while Hendrix strung his upside down, the two shallowest string grooves in the nut being filed to facilitate this. Two distinguishing marks on the fretboard were a lightning strike going through the fifth fret inlay and a Saturnlike ring around the seventeenth.

In the spirit of the times, and similar to Eric Clapton and George Harrison, Hendrix had his guitar refinished in a psychedelic pattern. Unlike them, however, he preferred to do the decoration himself, using swirling, psychedelic designs of hearts, flowers, leaves, kissing lips, and "love drops" in what appears to be nail polish.

It's probable the guitar was employed on his third album, *Electric Ladyland*, while some feel it could have featured as lead guitar on his hit Dylan cover, "All Along the Watchtower."

Its two powerful humbucking pickups added a different sound to Hendrix's tone palette alongside the single-coil Strat. The V was a similar weight to the Strat and easier to handle than a Les Paul, which he started using in May 1968—three months after he was last pictured with the V in San Francisco.

Notable Flying V players: Dave Davies (the Kinks); Tim Wheeler (Ash); Andy Powell (Wishbone Ash).

GIBSON FLYING V

Inspired by the then highly topical space race between the United States and the Soviet Union, the Gibson Flying V was introduced by Gibson back in the late 1950s. Its companion in the new "Modernistic" range was the similarly futuristic Explorer, the intention being to rival Fender's Strat and Jazzmaster that had left the Les Paul looking somewhat staid. (A third design, the Moderne, failed to make it to production.)

The V was to prove too unconventional for most and would only be produced in limited numbers until reintroduced some years later. Only ninety-eight originals were made, and these are now collectors' items: an additional twenty were assembled from parts in the early 1960s.

Control knobs on the scratch plate controlled the volume of the pickups (the selection switch was nearby) while there was a single master tone control. (The knobs were in line on early models but were rearranged in a triangle in the 1960s.) An arrowhead tailpiece anchored the strings while the jack plug was on the bottom of the lower horn. As ever with unusually shaped guitars, balance could be a problem, especially if played when seated.

Original Flying Vs were made of korina wood, had a string-through-body configuration, smooth neck joint, wider nut width, a slightly different body contour, and PAF pickups. The later mahogany-bodied V, as played by Hendrix, was manufactured between 1966 and 1970; the most significant of several differences was the added short Vibrola tailpiece.

Over time, pose appeal led to the Flying V's popularity among heavy metal guitarists, and also to its being copied by many other manufacturers, most notably Dean. In 1999 Gibson bowed to fashion with the Flying V Gothic, which featured black hardware.

A right-handed replica of Hendrix's decorated Flying V (right), modeled on the original (left), which was rediscovered in the late 1990s and restored to its former glory.

GIBSON LES PAUL

BIRTH OF AN ICON

Born in 1952, the Gibson Les Paul is now more than
half a century old, yet it is still an iconic instrument.
Guitarist and sound recording pioneer Les Paul had
been experimenting with a solid-bodied guitar
throughout the 1940s, mounting two homemade
pickups on a 4-by-4-inch cross-section pine "log" and
inserting it between two sawn-off halves of an
Epiphone guitar to make it more easily playable. The
objective was to reduce feedback, a by-product of
amplified acoustic guitars, and to better reproduce
tone. But it wasn't until the solid-body Telecaster
emerged from rival Fender's workshop that Gibson
expressed any interest in a production guitar.

   It was immediately popular, selling more than 2,000
copies in its first full year in the catalog. Its twin P-90

pickups—later replaced by humbuckers—and dense
body, a combination of mahogany with a maple top,
gave it an awesome sound. Cheaper versions like the
Junior would be introduced, but the Les Paul as
featured here is an industry standard, and many of
today's handmade "boutique" guitars reference it in
their design.

GOLDEN AGE

A Les Paul in sunburst finish as made available by
Gibson between 1958 and 1960 represents the Holy
Grail for rock guitar players. The highly figured maple
cap glued onto the heavy mahogany body is often seen
in "book-matched" form, the wood being split and the
grain pattern matched, making this variant even more
attractive. Aficionados know it as the Standard, though

that name never actually appeared on the guitar at the time; it was first referred to as such in Gibson literature in 1960, when buying one would have cost $280.

TUNE-O-MATIC

Amazingly for an iconic rock guitar, the solid-bodied twin-pickup Les Paul fell from favor in 1961, just under a decade after introduction. It was replaced by the less substantial SG, from which originator Les Paul distanced himself, and would not be revived by Gibson until Eric Clapton adopted the guitar for his classic recordings with John Mayall's Bluesbreakers on the so-called "Beano" album (*Blues Breakers with Eric Clapton*) of 1966. The model would not have been reinstated in production two years later without his intervention. The original Les Paul was the Goldtop, while the Custom, first introduced in 1954 as the deluxe version of the regular Les Paul, was also known as the "Fretless Wonder," a name which came from advertising claims that the frets were so low they gave a super-fast playing action. It was also first to feature the Tune-o-matic bridge with individual string intonation, which replaced the trapeze tailpiece and has remained a feature (with the separate tailpiece) ever since. The bridge, designed by Ted McCarty, allowed for individual intonation adjustment for each string. The humbucker pickups used in Les Pauls since 1957 were designed by Seth Lover and came to be known as PAF ("Patent Applied For"). The patent was granted in 1959, but the label has persisted until today.

The Les Paul Standard remains as perfect a guitar for rock as you could find—and genuine examples (as opposed to Slash's replica) dating from 1958 to 1960 in sunburst finish, nowadays command enormous sums.

The main image is a Gibson Les Paul from 1952 . Above, from left to right, a black Les Paul of 1982, a maple Les Paul of 1958, and a signature Jimmy Page Les Paul from 1998, complete with the Led Zeppelin guitarist's signature on the scratch plate.

GIBSON LES PAUL
PETER GREEN

Many would-be blues-meisters have emulated Fleetwood Mac founder Peter Green's style, but few have approached his instrumental eloquence. He succeeded Eric Clapton in John Mayall's Bluesbreakers in 1966 before leaving less than a year later to form Fleetwood Mac.

Green's one great advantage over his imitators was a 1959 Les Paul Standard, which he bought in the midsixties. It acquired its uniquely nasal tone by accident when he removed the pickups for rewinding and reinstalled one upside down, putting them permanently out of phase with each other. This has never been corrected for obvious reasons. The guitar's tone is highlighted on tracks like "The Supernatural," recorded with the Bluesbreakers on their one album on which he appeared, *A Hard Road*. The self-composed instrumental contained a series of sustained notes in a masterclass of controlled feedback that inspired Carlos Santana, three decades later, to use the title for his comeback album.

Fleetwood Mac's self-titled debut LP featured more of Green's inspired Les Paul playing. Onstage with the band, he used an Orange amplifier without any effects, though concert footage of the band shows them with Fender Dual Showman Reverb heads and matching 2-by-15-inch cabinets.

Up-and-coming Irish musician Gary Moore acquired Green's instrument around 1970 and used it on a tribute album, *Blues For Greeny*. After joining Moore onstage at the Shepherds Bush Empire in 1995 to take a well-deserved share of the applause, it was a short but significant step for Green—retired for a quarter of a century after mental health problems—to resume his own musical career.

Green's instrument of choice on his comeback was a semihollow Gibson Howard Roberts Fusion jazz guitar. In the 2000s he adopted a black Gibson Les Paul that was similar to his earlier trademark instrument.

The Les Paul's finish may have faded, as all sunbursts do, but Green's former guitar increased dramatically in value. It sold in March 2006 for a reported half-million dollars, the highest-priced example ever to change hands. While most often associated with classic rockers, Sex Pistol Steve Jones cranked out the three chords of 1977's "God Save the Queen" on a white Custom.

GIBSON LES PAUL
SLASH

Two decades after Eric Clapton and Peter Green, it was the equally inspirational image of Slash, Les Paul in hand and Marshall stack at his back, that led a generation of guitar players to tote a single-cutaway tobacco sunburst Standard.

Born Saul Hudson in Britain in 1965, Slash was the guitarist who helped Guns N' Roses explode onto the world stage in 1988. Pointed headstocks became passé overnight. "I didn't reintroduce the Les Paul," insisted a modest Slash. "I just don't think that anybody who was really popular and touring worldwide was using Les Pauls around the time Guns came out."

Slash was a guitar hero parachuted into a decade where, Van Halen apart, they'd been in exceedingly short supply. He was given his most famous Les Paul Standard by his manager during the *Appetite for Destruction* sessions, and went on to use it for much of *Use Your Illusion*, the Snakepit release, and two Velvet Revolver records. By creating an unforgettable intro, it propelled the anthemic "Sweet Child O' Mine" to the U.S. Number 1 spot in 1988, making Guns N' Roses only the fifth hard-rock band in history to top the singles chart.

He calls his mainstay recording guitar a "replica"—and he's technically right, as it was built by Chris Derrig as an exact replica of a late-1950s Standard, but with Seymour Duncan Alnico pickups. Gibson Slash signature models have been around for a decade now, but the man himself doesn't take his on the road anymore. "It's beat to shit, but it still sounds great!"

Though things went downhill after the initial breakthrough, Slash took two fellow Guns N' Roses members, replacement drummer Matt Sorum and Duff McKagan, to his next major

band, Velvet Revolver, where his sunburst Les Paul and top-hatted stage persona continued to entertain.

Notable Les Paul players: Billy Gibbons (ZZ Top); Joe Perry (Aerosmith); Tommy Bolin; Steve Hackett (Genesis); Neil Finn; the late Paul Kossoff (Free).

GIBSON LES PAUL JUNIOR
BILLIE JOE ARMSTRONG

The rise of Green Day from niche indie-rockers to international superstar status has been down to the singing and songwriting of Billie Joe Armstrong. The California trio struck gold in 1994 when their major-label debut, *Dookie*, broke through to the mainstream. It eventually sold more than 15 million worldwide. *American Idiot* (2004) re-established them as a band to watch after a relatively fallow period.

Armstrong began his career with a Stratocaster copy—the same type on which he had learned to play—named Blue from Japanese makers Fernandes. His current favored six-string guitar is the Gibson Les Paul Junior, a choice harking back to the British New Wave of the late 1970s, when Johnny Thunders and the Clash's Mick Jones used it. He scoured all the vintage stores and started a collection of about twenty—"everything from Specials to regular dog-ear (P-90) pickup to TV color to sunburst so I've pretty much got all the ones they made since 1955–1960....It's not just a collection, it's things that I actually put to use and play—they're not baseball cards." His favorite is the first, a 1956 example that he named Floyd. "I plugged it in and it was exactly the sound that had been in my head for so many years and then more. They have more

of a rock 'n' roll sound. That real punchy midrange sound."

With a solid mahogany body and neck and nickel hardware, the Billie Joe Armstrong Les Paul Junior, introduced in 2006, is based on Floyd. It combines the best features of a vintage Junior with a slim, tapered neck, as opposed to the notorious large neck or "baseball bat." It also has a specially designed H-90 pickup that is hum-canceling "so you can play it onstage and get just what the guitar sounds like." Armstrong's Les Paul Junior has featured on every Green Day album since 2000's *Warning*.

Notable Les Paul Junior players:
Leslie West (Mountain); Bob Marley; Peter Frampton; John Lennon.

GIBSON LES PAUL JUNIOR

The Les Paul Junior was marketed by Gibson as an ideal beginner's instrument when it first appeared in 1954. It was an uncontoured-body mahogany guitar, with a similar profile to its namesake, and featured a single P-90 pickup. The tailpiece was the standard stop bar as had just been introduced on its big brother, and its price tag on introduction was a modest $99. The Les Paul Special had a similar body shape but was equipped with two P-90 pickups and Gibson's standard four-knob, three-way switch electronics, while the Melody Maker, introduced in 1959, had a thinner headstock and double rather than single cutaway. The Junior was originally available in sunburst only, but the Les Paul TV boasted a natural finish similar to that of the Telecaster, which was reckoned to show up well on black-and-white television. The line was eventually folded into the SG family before disappearing quietly from Gibson's catalog in the late 1960s/early 1970s.

When punk arrived, Gibson's entry-level guitars like the Les Paul Junior and Melody Maker suddenly gained a new lease on life, being a cost-effective way to add guts to your sound. Epiphone, Gibson's budget arm, has offered cost-effective introductory Juniors that feature a bolt-on neck and a single humbucking pickup rather than the traditional P-90. Epiphone Japan has also released Juniors (with the Gibson headstock), including the LPJ-70 and the limited edition Lacquer Series Junior, made to the original 1954 Gibson specifications but for the Japanese market only.

The simple silhouette of the Les Paul Junior is all it shares with its more elaborate and expensive namesake, being lighter and thinner and having no "cap" to its body.

GIBSON SG COPY
FRANK ZAPPA

Frank Zappa's journey through guitars was as idiosyncratic as his music. He played a Gibson ES-5 Switchmaster on the first *Mothers of Invention* albums, but its classic-rock sound was not his preference. The next guitar to join Zappa's repertoire was a Gibson Les Paul Goldtop equipped with P-90 pickups. He used this guitar on his first solo album, *Hot Rats*, as well as on the song "Willie the Pimp." The guitar went through major modifications before Frank selected a modified Gibson SG with active circuits, various onboard preamps, and phase switching. This guitar was pictured on the cover of the *Roxy & Elsewhere* album.

Zappa acquired his trademark guitar by chance. An unknown fan came backstage in Phoenix, Arizona, in the 1970s and sold Frank a "Gibson SG" for $500. Closer inspection revealed some nonstandard Gibson features, the most visible a multiplicity of knobs and switches. Other features included ornamental woodwork and special inlays, including a star at the fifth fret and what appears to be eyes on the twelfth. The guitar also featured twenty-three frets instead of the usual twenty-two. The addition of this fret pushed the neck pickup back, resulting in a unique sound. The pickups are of unknown provenance. The guitar was once fit with a Vibrola-style tremolo before a stop-bar tailpiece was put in its place. Some features of the electronics of the guitar include a Dan Armstrong Green Ringer circuit, phase switching, an onboard preamp (added by luthier/electronics maker Rex Bogue), and maybe even coil-tapping switches. This guitar, along with a Pignose amp, was used to record *Overnite Sensation* and *Apostrophe*.

Notable Gibson SG players: Gary Rossington (Lynyrd Skynyrd); Tommy Iommi; Kelly Jones (Stereophonics); Angus Young; Robbie Krieger (the Doors); John Cipollina (Quicksilver Messenger Service).

GIBSON SG

Gibson unveiled the SG (Solid Guitar) series, with its angular design and pronounced double-cutaway profile, in 1959 as a replacement for the then-unfashionable Les Paul. The guitar retained Les Paul's name until 1963, when it was dropped (allegedly because he was divorcing wife Mary Ford and did not want his agreement with Gibson to be part of the proceedings). He also apparently did not like the design, saying, "A guy could kill himself on those sharp horns!" The body was by no means as substantial as the Les Paul, but like its predecessor was usually made of mahogany. It incurred lower production costs than that of the previous model, due to its one-piece body and flat rather than capped top. On the plus side, the neck, which merged into the body without a noticeable "heel," was substantially shallower and easier to play, and was advertised as the "fastest neck in the world." Various tailpiece and vibrato-system options were offered—again an advance on the Les Paul, which typically had only a stop tail.

The design would slowly gain in popularity in its own right as "name" players were seen with it through the 1960s. Also, the SG's double cutaway offered enhanced access to the higher frets than had the Les Paul. The SG was usually seen with two humbucking pickups, though a single P90 "dog-ear" was fit to the entry-level Junior. Most models had fancy trapezoidal fingerboard inlays rather than dots, though cheaper models would be introduced as time went by in the same way as the Les Paul begat the Junior. In 1966 the guitar was redesigned with a different neck joint, while a larger, semisymmetrical "bat-wing" pickguard appeared on 1967 models. In 1972 the neck was relocated further into the body, as the neck-body joint had been a notorious weak spot (as was the headstock, which was angled back to improve string tension over the nut). The SG remains in production today and is the choice of guitarists who enjoy its workmanlike, nonflashy qualities.

With three pickups, a single volume and tone control, and a "chicken-head" selector offering six pickup settings, this is a Gibson SG-3, claimed to take "the power, sustain, and tonal range of Gibson's legendary SG into new sonic dimensions."

GRETSCH 6120
BRIAN SETZER

When they exploded onto the music scene in 1980, the Stray Cats were a breath of fresh air. This American trio played no-nonsense, vintage rock 'n' roll, but like Jimi Hendrix before them, they had to cross the Atlantic Ocean to find an audience.

The seventeen-year-old Setzer idolized the late Eddie Cochran and chose a Gretsch 6120—previously adopted by Cochran, Duane Eddy,

and other rock 'n' roll/rockabilly pioneers—to be like his hero. "I had no idea what it was called but I knew I had to have one," he said. "When I was seventeen, I saw an ad in the paper. When I saw that it was an Eddie Cochran, I bought it on the spot for $100."

Just three years later, Setzer and his Stray Cats sparked a rockabilly revival in England, and they would soon do the same in the United States. He made virtually no modifications to the guitar, though he did personalize it with stickers of 1950s pinup girls and dice instead of control knobs. "My only real modification to the guitar was putting Sperzel locking tuners on: when the band got serious, I realized that I had to play in tune. The pickups are stock Gretsch FilterTrons, they've always sounded fantastic."

The Gretsch can be heard on the first single, "Runaway Boys," and subsequent hits "Rock This Town," "Stray Cat Strut," and "The Race Is On." In the same year that the band split up, 1984, the original 6120 was replaced. "It had beer spilled on it and smoke blown all over it; it was beat on pretty badly. In about 1984, I ran into Steve Miller in a bar in Germany. We talked about Gretsches and how mine was getting trashed. When I got back to New York there was a big box waiting for me, and, to my delighted surprise, it was a 6120 from Steve Miller. Not just a 6120, but a great one!"

Setzer now has his own Gretsch signature models: the Brian Setzer Nashville and Hot Rod (using Hot Rod FilterTron or TV Jones pickups) are derivatives of the 6120, while the Black Phoenix is a take on the White Falcon.

Notable Gretsch 6120 players:
Bryan Adams' guitarist Keith Scott; Bo Diddley; Chet Atkins.

GRETSCH 6120

Fred Gretsch marketed his first semi-acoustic guitars in 1951. Input from Nashville guitar great Chet Atkins helped make the 6120, for most players, the ultimate Gretsch classic, while more publicity came from bluesman Bo Diddley and his distinctive rectangular guitar.

In many respects, Gretsch was ahead of its competitors. The Synchro-Sonic bridge allowing for individual string intonation was on the market before Gibson's acclaimed Tune-o-matic, while the Gretsch humbucking pickup, named the FilterTron, was developed before Gibson's PAF, even though both appeared simultaneously.

In the mid-1960s, the name of the 6120 changed from its original name, 6120 Chet Atkins Hollow Body, to 6120 Nashville, but the first name was restored and is now in use. Decorations on the 6120 included a Gretsch "G" mark, as if the wood had been branded like cattle hide.

Fred Gretsch left the company that bore his name in 1971, but his nephew, also Fred, bought the business back from new owners Baldwin in 1989. Production of the 6120 had stopped in the late 1970s, when quality control issues devalued the brand. But when Brian Setzer was seen playing an old 6120 in his early-1980s music videos, Gretsch decided to re-enter the guitar business. At the start of 2003, Fender took responsibility for all aspects of Gretsch's guitars and basses.

The Gretsch 6120 has no lack of distinguishing features. The horseshoe motif on the headstock was introduced in 1956.

GRETSCH DUO JET
GEORGE HARRISON

When, in the spring of 1964, Beatle George Harrison played a Gretsch Country Gentleman on *The Ed Sullivan Show*, the number of these guitars sold in the following twelve-month period jumped to more than 2,000. It showed just how influential the band had become in the few short years since 1961, when Harrison had bought the guitar's predecessor, a solid-bodied, single-cutaway Gretsch Duo Jet.

It had been made in 1957 and he had seen

it advertised in the *Liverpool Echo* newspaper by a merchant seaman who'd imported it privately from the United States. It certainly beat the Czech-made Futurama he'd been struggling with. He called it "my first good guitar....I was so proud to own that." Harrison was pictured playing it at the Cavern Club in July 1961. He played it through a Gibson GA-40 Les Paul amplifier, with no effects.

The Duo Jet had been used to great purpose by Gene Vincent's first guitarist, Cliff Gallup, and, with American-made guitars both scarce and unaffordable, the £75 George had saved up from gigs to buy it seems a bargain.

Color aside, Gretsch Jet guitars are all virtually identical. The Duo Jet was black, the Fire Bird was a deep red, and the Silver Jet was covered in silver-sparkle plastic-drum material.

George's Duo Jet can be heard on recordings like "Love Me Do" and cuts from the Beatles' first album, *Please Please Me*. By the summer of 1963 he had graduated to the larger, semi-acoustic Country Gentleman. The fact he'd used the Duo Jet more or less every night in the group's early days was proven by wear lines on the back of the clear-finished mahogany neck.

The guitar that started a love affair with Gretsch that lasted till the end of Harrison's life has recently gained a new lease on life through the computer game, The Beatles: Rock Band, which offers a selection of "authentic" instruments to act as "controllers."

When playing with the Raconteurs, Jack White usually plays two custom copies of the Duo Jet, one of which, dubbed the Triple Jet, is made of copper.

GRETSCH DUO JET

The stringed instruments manufactured by drum manufacturer Fred Gretsch were favored by some of rock's earliest pioneers, such as Eddie Cochran. This encouraged Gretsch to offer ever more sophisticated designs. While top-of-the-line guitars like the White Falcon and Chet Atkins grabbed the headlines, the relatively straightforward Duo Jet was an effective weapon in any 1960s beat merchant's arsenal.

Gretsch had introduced it in 1953 to counter the success of the Gibson Les Paul, whose silhouette it superficially resembled. Fred Gretsch considered it a comedown, declaring that "anybody with a band-saw and a router can make a solid-body guitar."

Unlike the heavy Gibson, its mahogany body was only semisolid, offering a welcome weight saving. The separate pieces of mahogany used had to accommodate many routed channels for wiring and components before a pressed, arched top was added. The neck was also thinner and more comfortable to play

than the Les Paul's "clubby" profile. Interestingly, it retailed at $230, $5 more than its rival. Also the Melita Synchro-Sonic bridge allowed individual string intonation, beating Gibson's Tune-o-matic into production by a year.

The distinctive knobs and Gretsch-branded Bigsby vibrato gave the Duo Jet, presumably named for its two FilterTron pickups, an expensive look, paralleled by the relatively elaborate fretboard inlays. The controls were potentially confusing, however: each of the two pickups had a volume knob, the third of the triangle being a three-way selector switch for changing the frequency output of the guitar. Then a Gibson-style pickup selector switch sat on the upper horn with a master-volume knob on the lower. Aficionados claimed this allowed more subtle sound selection: many a youngster might have been bamboozled.

This modern Duo Jet reissue lacks conventional fretboard inlays, these being fingernail-sized and at the top, not center, of the board, as in George Harrison's case.

GRETSCH WHITE FALCON
NEIL YOUNG

Canadian Neil Young first found global fame collaborating with early-1970s supergroup Crosby, Stills & Nash. As a solo artist his career has successfully combined the facets of acoustic singer-songwriter (as perfected on 1972's *Harvest*) and electric rock 'n' roller (1978's *Rust Never Sleeps*).

When not using his black Les Paul in the latter incarnation, he can be seen using a Gretsch White Falcon. He shares his fanaticism for the instrument with Stephen Stills. Young used a late-1950s single-cutaway model—the Holy Grail for collectors—when he

first linked with Stills in pre–Crosby, Stills, Nash & Young (CSNY) band Buffalo Springfield, the pair buying White Falcons to celebrate signing a record contract. The Springfield's biggest hit, "For What It's Worth," had two dominant background harmonic notes throughout the song, played by Young on a White Falcon with subtle use of the Bigsby vibrato/tremolo. Neil traded his mono 6136 to Stills for a stereo model 6137 White Falcon—the second version Gretsch produced. It is supposedly the only time he has ever parted with a guitar in his career. At times in the early 1970s,

GRETSCH WHITE FALCON

The top-of-the-line Gretsch White Falcon of 1955 was not one of the company's more popular models, partly because of its $600 price tag. This was the era of the flash automobile; the Cadillacs and Lincolns of the day influenced design in many mediums. And the White Falcon certainly had looks on its side. Everything (except the black DeArmond pickups and ebony fingerboard) was either white or gold. All edges—top, sides, back, f-holes, fingerboard, and headstock—were bound in gold, while the pickguard was gold-tinted plastic with an engraved falcon. Even the pearl fingerboard inlays had a falcon wing etched into them.

In place of the company's standard tailpiece with the letter *G* cut out, Gretsch substituted a new gold-plated model with the *G* now between two tubular members and a V-shaped piece at the string mounts. The Falcon's headstock design was also distinctively different, echoing the tailpiece by dipping to form a V-shape. The Gretsch logo was inlaid vertically in gold-sparkle material, while lightning bolts extended from both sides of the G.

The Falcon's design changed over time; in 1958 it added FilterTron pickups and thumbprint-style inlays, while the body acquired a double cutaway in the early 1960s—the single cut would return as an option in 1975. Sadly, the Falcon's unique vertical Gretsch logo was replaced by the standard straight-across logo in 1959.

In 1959, Gretsch also offered a White Falcon with separate channels for bass and treble, while the mid-1960s Stereo Falcon boasted no fewer than ten knobs and switches.

Fender Musical Instruments took control of Gretsch's manufacturing and distribution in 2002. Despite their changing hands, the new White Falcons are said to be as good as vintage models and are flying off the shelves.

Everything about the Gretsch White Falcon screams class. This one (right) has a tremolo arm shaped like a steer's antlers.

CSNY had as many as three White Falcons onstage at the same time. And the 2002 spring tour of the U.S. of the re-formed CSNY saw Stills and Young playing White Falcons on classic numbers like "Southern Man" and "Cinnamon Girl." He also played the instrument on the studio recording of "Ohio," the song about the killing of four students at Kent State University in 1970.

Young's favored guitar/amp combination is achieved by playing his Gretsch through a blond Fender Deluxe.

Notable White Falcon players: Randy Bachman, whose collection rivals that fellow Canadian Young; Billy Duffy (the Cult); Charlie Burchill (Simple Minds).

HAMER PROTOTYPE
ANDY SUMMERS

Andy Summers used many different guitars in his long career, which began in the 1960s when he played with bands as diverse in style as the Animals and Soft Machine. By the time he was co-opted into the Police, replacing original guitarist Henri Padovani, he had settled on a Fender Telecaster, which he had modified with a humbucking pickup in the neck position.

But as the Police advanced toward international superstardom—thanks to Sting's

vocal and songwriting skills, Summers's effects-laden guitar work, and Stewart Copeland's ferocious percussion—he was approached by Jol Danzig of Hamer guitars.

The Prototype (confusingly, the name of the model) was launched at Madison Square Garden in late 1980 and was unusual in including both a humbucker and single-coil pickup on the same guitar, like Summers's modified Telecaster. This allowed heavier, rockier sounds to be extracted while retaining the single-coil bridge pickup's scratchy tone. A limited number of twelve-string versions were also built.

The first Prototype, identifiable by its abbreviated pickguard, had been taken by Jol Danzig to New York the day before the show. After the instrument was broken in transit by the airline, Danzig used a Forty-eighth Street guitar repair shop to make it playable again.

Summers upgraded to a Hamer Phantom in 1983, which added a neck pickup to the Prototype. This allowed him to get the "in-between" sounds of a Strat along with humbucking tones. This was one of the industry's first Superstrat-type designs. His version had three interchangeable magnetic fingerboards— regular fretted, modal fretted, and fretless. Summers played them on the Synchronicity Tour that effectively ended the Police story; that is, until their reformation in 2007.

Notable Hamer players: Rick Nielson (Cheap Trick); Steve Stevens (for Billy Idol).

HAMER PROTOTYPE

Hamer Guitars was established in Illinois in 1975 by Paul Hamer and Jol Danzig. The Hamer Prototype was the first completely original design to be put into full production. Honduras mahogany was used for the body and glued-in set neck. The body shape was contoured in the back and front with unequal cutaways. A two-ply scratch plate (inscribed with the Prototype name) hid the neck joint, no neck pickup being fit.

Contemporary advertising made much of the new design triple-coil pickup, nicknamed the Motherbucker. But this was in fact two pickups sandwiched together, a DiMarzio PAF nearest the bridge in the same mounting as a single coil from the same maker. A three-way switch selected the humbucker, the single coil or both pickups simultaneously; a master volume and master tone control completed the electronics.

Paul Hamer claimed it was possible "to get anything from a sharp Stratocaster tone to a richer Les Paul sound with a good midrange Hamer sound in between." He credited Andy Summers with some of the design input in the same interview.

The Hamer Phantom was based in part on the Cruise Bass but shared many features with the Prototype. A second scratch-plate-mounted single-coil pickup was added, and most pickup combinations were possible. The Phantom A5 deviated further from the Prototype, losing the three-a-side headstock in favor of a new six-on-a-side design and Kahler locking tremolo.

The company was taken over by Ovation owner Kaman in 1988, and subsequent designs tended toward the ubiquitous Superstrat model.

This Prototype (right) differs from Andy Summers's in appearing to have a Seymour Duncan humbucker in place of the original cream DiMarzio, plus an extra switch, which presumably operates a coil tap on the humbucker.

HÖFNER VIOLIN BASS
PAUL McCARTNEY

It's ironic that Paul McCartney, the most influential rock and pop bass player outside of the United States, never regularly used a Fender. It's certain that his style shaped generations that followed, yet his first serious bass (and the one with which he remains connected to this day) was a relatively cheap German instrument.

The small-bodied, semi-acoustic Höfner Violin Bass was his choice initially because, being left-handed, he could turn a right-handed version over and play it "without looking stupid." American guitars were hard to get hold of in the U.K.'s postwar austerity years. People were dissuaded from buying imported goods, especially American-made luxury items like guitars.

McCartney bought his Höfner 500/1 in Hamburg during the Beatles' second Star Club

HÖFNER VIOLIN BASS

Karl Höfner began his musical instrument company in 1887, manufacturing violins, cellos, and basses, but did not begin making guitars until 1949. Prior to 1958, Höfners were only seen outside Germany through servicemen returning to the U.K. or groups returning from Hamburg nightclubs, but from 1958 the Selmer Company imported their products and they were more widely seen.

Amazingly, the "Beatle" bass was not included in Selmer's catalog until 1963, when the band's popularity had stimulated demand. Even then the instruments were hand-built, as Höfner refused to change their traditional production methods to keep up.

The 500/1 had been unveiled in 1956, and its shape made it a close relation of Höfner's early products. In fact it was a scaled-down bass viola body, without the usual f-holes, fitted with a twenty-two-fret guitar neck. It was considerably lighter than Gibson's EB-0 bass, which it resembled, as the American guitar was solid bodied.

Two oval pickups were both originally situated next to the neck, but they were soon moved apart for tonal variation. The oval control plate of the early model was also changed to the now-familiar rectangular version.

In 1961, the company name was added to the headstock and more efficient metal-cased pickups fitted, completing the bass Paul McCartney is now identified with. In 1968 a deluxe "Super Beatle" model was introduced with a flamed maple back and rims, a spruce top, elaborate bindings, pearl fingerboard inlays, and gold hardware.

The Höfner Violin Bass (left) retains its popularity in the current century, despite many disadvantages when compared with solid-bodied basses.

sojourn there in 1961. "Fenders were around £100, even then, and all I could afford was about £30," confesses the current multi-millionaire. He would continue using the instrument until the Beatles retired from touring in 1966 (a nod to its lightness, which allowed him to move around the stage relatively unhindered).

He also believed the light weight of the hollow-bodied instrument encouraged him to "play more melodic riffs…kind of guitar parts really." Its tone was pleasingly "like a string bass sometimes," and its main drawback was "inaccuracy of tuning when you get up the neck a bit." Nevertheless it featured on such albums as *A Hard Day's Night*, *Beatles for Sale*, and *Rubber Soul*. The success of the band

prompted Merseybeat rivals the Searchers to invest in one.

McCartney moved on to the Rickenbacker 4001 in 1967, the year the Beatles produced their legendary studio creation *Sgt. Pepper's Lonely Hearts Club Band*. He could now, of course, afford left-handed instruments, which, by that time, were readily available even to U.K. players. With McCartney leading the way, bass players were now appreciating that they could make musical things happen instead of having to tag along underneath and play the root notes of each and every chord. No longer would the bass player necessarily be the least able guitarist, but now he could cut loose and play countermelodies. So the homely Höfner had helped play a part in a revolution.

IBANEZ JEM
STEVE VAI

If Eddie Van Halen prepared the ground for an 1980s guitar revival, then Steve Vai, along with sometime teacher Joe Satriani, was responsible for igniting the rock scene in his wake. Their style, extremely fast, flowing, and technical, became known as "shredding."

Vai, born in New York in 1960, first came to attention as a member of Frank Zappa's band when he was just nineteen years old. From 1979 to 1984, he performed on many Zappa albums including *Shut Up 'n Play Yer Guitar* and *You Are What You Is*. He released his first solo album, *Flex-Able*, in 1984; he joined heavy-

metal band Alcatrazz in 1985; and in 1986 he made a scene-stealing cameo appearance in the movie *Crossroads*.

A string of solo albums have since added luster to the legend as Vai's instrumental shredding won him a generation of young acolytes. Current guitar idols like James "Munky" Shaffer of Korn, Mike Eizinger of Incubus, and Tom Morello of Audioslave all cite him as a major inspiration.

Ibanez identified Vai as a major player and built him a prototype guitar with the pickup configuration he favored, a palm rest for the tremolo, and a red and grey snakeskin finish. They sent it to him for Christmas 1986, and the response was so positive that within three months he and Ibanez had completed a new model, the JEM. His last pre-Ibanez guitar had

been made by L.A. guitar builder Tom Anderson. "I took the best of the sounds ... and had them incorporated into the Ibanez," he said in 1988.

Vai can be heard playing his signature Ibanez JEM on former Van Halen frontman David Lee Roth's 1988 release *Skyscraper*, as well as on his own solo release, *Passion and Warfare*. He has used the JEM on every record since.

The JEM, says Vai, is "a very fine instrument that will transcend my popularity as a guitarist. As time goes on and other great guitar players some along, I don't think the guitar will bow out, because it's a good guitar and it should live on." His link with Ibanez had been the most influential "signature deal" in a decade.

IBANEZ JEM

The first Ibanez instruments appeared in Japan as long ago as 1932, but it took four decades for them to reach the outside world, initially with copies of the Gibson SG and Les Paul and then Fender clones. The push toward original designs began when, in 1977, Gibson sued Ibanez for infringement of their copyright.

Their first major solid design, the Destroyer, was tied in with Kiss's Paul Stanley, an endorsement that led to many fans like Eddie Van Halen purchasing the instrument. Steve Vai was the next endorsee, 1987's JEM range of guitars, reflecting his wish for a Stratlike body shape and "pointy" headstock—not to mention a gimmicky scalloped crescent-moon carrying handle, or "monkey grip."

Two prototypes were made from Vai's plans. The first was a semihollow body, made out of maple, with a maple neck. The second one was maple/mahogany/maple with a solid body. Both incorporated the "monkey grip" and housed two DiMarzio PAF Pro 151 humbucking pickups and one DiMarzio

custom-wound single coil. It was right for the time, as the Superstrat concept of humbucker-equipped Stratocaster-shaped guitars had been fueled by L.A. "hair bands" who flocked to Charvel/Jackson and Kramer guitars.

Vai sent the maple one back with instructions that the 21st, 22nd, 23rd, and 24th frets were to be scalloped, to give increased access. He liked the maple neck but wanted a rosewood fingerboard. A major change was to make the bodies out of much lighter basswood.

Many JEM features have since been incorporated into Ibanez's RG range and the RG550 is considered one of the definitive modern rock guitars.

Aside from the distinctive "monkey grip" cutout and pointed headstock, a recognition feature of the Ibanez, JEM is the locking tremolo with fine-tuning keys.

JACKSON PC1
PHIL COLLEN

London-born Phil Collen was brought into the ranks of Sheffield metallurgists Def Leppard in 1983, replacing Pete Willis as a foil to the flamboyant Steve Clark. The pair became known as the Terror Twins, though Collen retreated from the rock lifestyle and gave up alcohol and meat. But Clark's continuing substance abuse left Collen the focus of attention: he recorded all the guitar parts of 1991's *Adrenalize* after Clark's sudden death, and he was the senior partner to Viv

Campbell thereafter. To celebrate completing the *Adrenalize* album, Jackson made him a guitar with the album art as its finish.

Previously an endorsee of Ibanez Destroyer guitars, Collen teamed with Jackson in 1989 to develop an "ergonomically correct" electric guitar called the PC Archtop.

Collen had been using various custom Jackson Soloists over the previous three years, and has since designed three more models, known as the PC1, 2, and 3, with the reverse headstock a distinguishing feature. His main stage guitar is a PC1, "a real hot rod." Known as Dread, it is a mahogany and maple PC1, "with a paint job of a monster with all of these dreadlocks and it glows in the dark. It's green and when the lights go off, it just lights up."

The PC1 has a fat neck, which Collen believes helps obtain fatter and bigger tone. He uses heavy .13–.54-gauge (0.013–0.054-inch) strings on all his guitars—"I really dig into it and attack it"—while he tunes down to E flat in common with many metal guitarists. Stretching strings before use is an absolute necessity for Collen's favored combo of very heavy strings with a Floyd Rose tremolo system. The Floyd Rose has titanium saddle pieces and tremolo blocks, which gives more sustain without being overly bright or brittle: very defined, but not sharp or harsh-sounding.

Notable Jackson players: Dave Mustaine (Megadeth); Jeff Beck; Randy Rhoads.

JACKSON PC1

Guitar maker Grover Jackson, who bought out Charvel in 1978, had always focused on the higher-profile end of the metal market. Outstanding young guitarist Randy Rhoads—soon to link with Ozzy Osbourne and tragically die when an on-the-road prank went wrong—was heavily involved in his designs. Charvel guitars were based on the Fender Strat with bolt-on necks, while the Jackson guitars had more unique body shapes and neck-through-body construction. Jacksons featured eye-catching body shapes and angled, pointy headstocks.

Phil Collen's signature PC1 was one of the original Jackson signature guitars; it was based on the Dinky model but featured more exotic woods and the Jackson sustainer/driver system. It exists in five different models, currently produced and sold through Jackson, and could accurately be described as a Superstrat.

The production PC1 boasts a quilted maple top and compound-radius flame fretboard to provide visual appeal. The pickup combination is a double-bladed battery-powered sustainer humbucker at the neck with a DiMarzio HS2 in the middle and DiMarzio Super 3 at the bridge; the latter two are used to "dish out that signature Phil Collen chunk and screaming sustain." Its mahogany body is mounted by a Floyd Rose double-locking tremolo, while the bolt-on maple neck is quartersawn. The deep body cutaways allow access to the twenty-fourth fret.

In 1997, Japan's Arai (makers of the Aria range) acquired Jackson/Charvel, leading to the retirement of the latter name but a continued future for the company. It was later purchased by Fender, who also own Charvel.

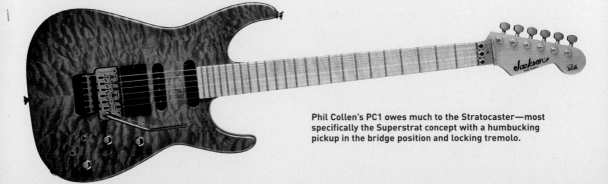

Phil Collen's PC1 owes much to the Stratocaster—most specifically the Superstrat concept with a humbucking pickup in the bridge position and locking tremolo.

JACKSON RANDY RHOADS
RANDY RHOADS

Randy Rhoads was a guitar hero cut down senselessly in his prime. At age fourteen he formed Violet Fox with his older brother Kelle and, two years later, formed Quiet Riot with vocalist Kevin DuBrow. Discouraged by major-label disinterest, he moved on to Ozzy's employ in 1979. He appeared on and toured the albums *Blizzard of Oz* and *Diary of a Madman*. After a March 1982 gig in Tennessee, the band's tour-bus driver took him up for a flight in his lightplane. While following the tour bus the plane crashed, killing all onboard.

Originally a Les Paul fan—he had two Customs, cream and black examples dating from 1975 and 1957 respectively—Rhoads played through Marshall Super Lead 100-watt head and Marshall 4-by-12-inch cabinets. Effects included wah-wah, flanger, chorus, phaser, and an echo unit. He abandoned Gibson for Jackson when they created a signature model for him, but he died before the guitar went into mass production.

James Hetfield, Dweezil Zappa, Buckethead, and John Petrucci are among a generation of guitarists for whom Rhoads was a guiding light, while Vinnie Vincent of Kiss was first to be offered the signature guitar by Jackson after Rhoads's death.

Interestingly, weeks before his passing, Rhoads had expressed interest in quitting rock to pursue a degree in classical guitar

JACKSON RANDY RHOADS

In December 1980 Randy Rhoads approached Grover Jackson of Charvel guitars with a design idea based on the classic Gibson Flying V. The white-with-black-pinstripe guitar that was the first to bear the Jackson name was sent to Rhoads in England about two months later. Known as "the Original Sin," this was played on the Ozzy Osbourne *Diary of a Madman* album.

In 1981 Rhoads and Jackson devised the Sharkfin body shape, which helped to differentiate his white Jackson from the standard Flying V. He wanted something more distinctive, and this was achieved by making the upper wing of the guitar thicker and more elongated.

Rhoads would receive this black-bodied silver pickguard guitar, the second Jackson ever made, just before the start of the Diary of a Madman tour. This was the Jackson Randy Rhoads, though the modest guitarist wanted to call it the Concorde. Like its predecessor it had a maple through neck and a string-through-body bridge. In production it proved a very popular model that put the Jackson name on the map.

This guitar features Grover locking tuners, a pair of Seymour Duncan humbucking pickups, a TB-4 (bridge) and an SH-2 (neck), and a Floyd Rose or Jackson Low Profile tremolo. The compound-radius rosewood fingerboard has flattened frets to facilitate playing fast and usually has twenty-two frets, though it's also available as a twenty-four-fret model for extra range.

Jackson would later team the Randy Rhoads neck and pointed headstock with a Fender-shaped body to create the highly successful Soloist, widely acknowledged as the first Superstrat.

The angular Jackson Randy Rhoads (right), a popular variation on Gibson's original Flying V concept. Unusually, this very attractive example has no tremolo.

JAYDEE CUSTOM BASS
MARK KING

Briton Mark King was pop music's preeminent bass player of the 1980s, incorporating the slap-and-pop style first popularized in 1970s disco into his band's sound. He made the bass guitar a lead instrument but only took up the bass after having to sell his drum kit on an ill-fated trip to Austria, when he needed the money to pay for a ticket home.

His jazz-funk band Level 42 emerged from the U.K.'s Isle of Wight to become an unlikely chart force. The first JayDee bass to be owned by King was reviewed in *International Musician*

and *Recording World* magazine in 1980. The following year it was bought by King in a shop in Shaftsbury Avenue, London, where its maker had put it on consignment.

King owned at least ten JayDee basses, the others made to his specifications; but in 1997 he underwent a personal catharsis and disposed of many. The two instruments he kept were "my first ever JayDee and another lovely JayDee that John (Diggins) made for my birthday around four years ago." This was produced with book-matched quilted maple front and back. He went on to use Status Graphite basses and in 2000 helped develop the Status KingBass, a headless, double-cutaway bass with a woven graphite through neck.

The band split in 1994 and King took time out from music, but he won the rights to use the name eight years later and still tours as Level 42 today. He has played on sessions with many other U.K. artists, but his influence on four-stringers the world over is his biggest legacy.

JAYDEE CUSTOM BASS

The man behind the JayDee marque was John Diggins, a former employee of guitar maker John Birch. The name "JayDee" is phonetic for his initials, and the instrument Mark King initially popularized was from the first batch of six basses he made. Diggins was heavily influenced by the design of Alembic high-end basses in the States. Some of his instruments had mahogany bodies with laminated centers.

Diggins had been involved in the design of Slade's "Super Yob" and the Glitter Band's "Star Guitar," and he was very much into taking the visual aspect of guitar design and applying it to the relatively unfashionable four string. He liked shapes that looked good—hence the crescent-shaped fretboard inlays and round string retainers that made his designs instantly identifiable.

The first JayDee as purchased by Mark King "had originally been made for another bass player in the U.S. but because he didn't want to pay for it, I finished it anyway." It boasted then-unique finishing touches like Saturn-shaped fretboard inlays, rosewood control knobs, brass hardware, and one of the first active electronic circuits to be found in a British-made bass. The idea of spraying it cherry red on one side came in a moment of inspiration and, like the other features, would become a trademark.

The multiplicity of knobs on a JayDee reflects a three-band EQ system, with tone knobs for treble, mid, and bass. The grooved wooden pickup covers deflect damage caused by "slapping."

LAKLAND BASS
ADAM CLAYTON

As with so many New Wave musicians, Adam Clayton, the bass player of U2, developed his skills on the job. But he had played in a band before, so he had the advantage over his colleagues. Singer Bono recalled in 1981 that Adam used to "pretend he could play bass. He came round and started using words like action and fret and he had us baffled. He had the only amplifier, so we never argued with him. We thought this guy must be a musician, he knows what he's talking about and then one day we discovered he wasn't playing the right notes!"

Clayton was an Ibanez endorser in the 1980s, playing their Musician model. But after playing Live Aid in 1985 the band sold the instruments used at the charity show,

including his Ibanez. After that he began using a Fender Jazz.

During the Elevation Tour in 2001, Clayton had switched to Lakland and used two U.S.-made Joe Osborn signature models—one sunburst, one natural—and a Bob Glaub signature, also in natural finish.

U2's Dublin base, Hanover Quay, was flooded in the spring of 2002 when the band members were in Los Angeles for the Grammy Awards. The first-floor storage area was breached and band members' equipment lost. Which of Clayton's basses were destroyed is uncertain, but he reverted to the Fender Jazz Bass shortly thereafter. He would return to Lakland bass guitars in 2005, using four examples of the Darryl Jones. Two were in natural finish with custom black blocks, one in metallic teal green with custom abalone blocks and one gold with custom abalone blocks; all had maple necks.

Notable Lakland players: John McVie (Fleetwood Mac); Jason Scheff (Chicago); Donald "Duck" Dunn.

LAKLAND BASS

Lakland was formed in 1995 by American luthier Paul Lakin with partner Hugh McFarland. Though it has created original designs, the company spent much time "improving" the Fender Precision and Jazz Bass designs. In many cases it has produced signature models for noted U.S. musicians, and their reputations have helped spread the company's name.

Their basses came with graphite-reinforced maple necks featuring rosewood, maple, or ebony fingerboards; solid alder or ash bodies; active Bartolini humbucking pickups (since replaced by similar-type pickups of Lakland's own manufacture); and three-band active equalization, in four- and five-string versions, fretted and fretless. Some models are available with a pickguard and Seymour Duncan Basslines pickups. The Lakland Darryl Jones model is an extrapolation of the Fender Jazz concept, made to the specification of the man who took over for Bill Wyman with the Rolling Stones. It has a slightly smaller body and was originally designed in 1995 by Albey Balgochian. The first attempt, known as the A-Bass, was road tested on the last year of the Stones' Bridges to Babylon tour.

Lakland commented that "the Darryl Jones Signature bass looks similar to our Osborn models, but has more curve to its contouring and dramatic cutaways that add to its vintage styling. Darryl personally selected a pair of passive J-bass pickups designed by Aero Instrument." Three knobs control tone, bridge volume, and neck volume. Jones has now transferred his endorsement to another company, but the design remains a modern classic.

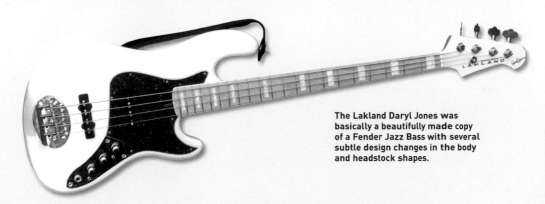

The Lakland Daryl Jones was basically a beautifully made copy of a Fender Jazz Bass with several subtle design changes in the body and headstock shapes.

MANSON MB-1
MATT BELLAMY

Few modern-day guitarists have gained more plaudits in the last decade than Matt Bellamy. The Muse frontman has tantalized the eardrums on lead guitar since the band's debut album, *Showbiz*, in 1999. He is known for his long association with Manson guitars; hailing from Devon, he collaborates closely with Exeter native Hugh Manson on a string of custom guitars that help him achieve his distinctive sound.

But it was a Peavey EVH Wolfgang, one of the designs endorsed by U.S. guitar hero Eddie Van Halen, that Bellamy started out with when Muse debuted in 1999; he customized this in curious fashion with gray gaffa tape on its top edge, and it survived the album's tour before it was launched into the crowd. A Parker Fly,

made from futuristic composite materials like resin and carbon glass, has also since been seen in his hands.

When touring the second album, *Origin of Symmetry*, and later *Absolution*, Bellamy's weapon of choice was his Manson Delorean, which can be heard on the opening riff of "Plug In Baby," which has come first in many of the polls to find the riff of a decade.

The world tour for *Black Holes and Revelations* saw Bellamy use a MIDI Manson. This mirror-plated guitar contained an integrated Kaoss Pad, which allows him to reproduce the DJ-scratch section from "Supermassive Black Hole." The pad is also used to control his Digitech Whammy effects pedal, ensuring maximum output through minimum effort.

The MIDI Manson, which became a Bellamy trademark, met its end at the Fuji Rock Festival in Naeba, Japan; at the conclusion of "Stockholm Syndrome," Bellamy launched the custom instrument at a strobe light, splitting it in half. It now resides at its maker's Exeter shop. Few guitars survive in Bellamy's guitar locker for more than a few years, but he plays them all with the same vigor and mesmerizing results. His innovation in conjunction with Manson has been a major factor in his and Muse's success over the last ten years.

MANSON MB-1

Matt Bellamy's association with Hugh Manson culminated in the release of Bellamy's signature guitar, the Manson MB-1. Based on his main guitar, the MB-1 had a solid alder body, with a bird's-eye maple neck—sturdy, but still not guaranteed to survive the impact Bellamy subjects it to during a gig. It has an exclusive

Manson MBK-2 Bridge pickup and a Fernandes Sustainer humbucker at the neck, the combination creating sustained crisp notes typical of a Muse track. Below the bridge is an X-Y MIDI pad, incorporated on all Bellamy's guitars since 2006. With it he can control a Kaoss Pad, allowing countless more sounds to emanate from his guitar. This touchpad MIDI controller, sampler, and effects processor is made by Korg. Its internal effects engine can be applied to a line-in signal or to samples recorded from the line-in. Effects available include pitch shifting, distortion, filtering, wah-wah, tremolo, flanging, delay, reverberation, autopanning, gating phasing, and ring modulation.

Visually, the MB-1 comes either matte black, or as Bellamy prefers, gloss red glitter. Manson recalls Bellamy's initial request: "I asked him to write down what he wanted, and he wrote 'sparkles.' When I was making it, I used a, well, it was like a wheat sifter, and just put the glitter on a bit at a time, then blew off the extra. It reminded me of making Christmas cards!"

Similar to a Telecaster in profile, the Manson MB-1 reflects the demands of the guitarist whose initials it bears. Switches include two that control the Fernandes sustainer pickup at the neck and a "kill switch" to turn off sound completely.

MARTIN D-28
JOHN MARTYN

John Martyn, born Iain McGeachy in Surrey in 1948, was the first white artist signed to the Island label. He was a master of the acoustic guitar yet refused to restrict himself: Gibsons were as dear to him as his two Martin acoustics. Listening to The Band converted him to electricity. But it was when, in the early 1970s, he started applying the kind of effects to his acoustic that had previously been restricted to the electric that he truly

broke new ground. The catalyst was jazz saxophonist Pharoah Sanders, whose *Karma* album Martyn heard at the impressionable age of twenty-one. "I'd never heard someone play so emotionally...with that sense of humanity." He bought an Echoplex tape-loop echo effect in an attempt to imitate Sanders's sustain on his guitar. A voyage of discovery in sound was beginning.

His 1971 *Bless the Weather* set the tone by being largely written in the studio and

MARTIN D-28

Founded in 1833 when Christian Freidrich Martin moved from the violin-making town of Markneukirchen in Saxony to Nazareth in Pennsylvania, the CF Martin company has dominated the acoustic guitar market since introducing the D-28 in 1931. Prior to this, Martin's main innovation had been to introduce the fourteen-fret neck, which allowed a greater range of notes and which was intended to appeal to plectrum banjo players. It also concentrated on steel rather than gut-string guitars, its X-bracing system making Martin instruments sturdy enough to withstand the extra stresses involved.

The D-28 was a Dreadnought guitar, named after a particularly capable class of Royal Navy battleship. This

had a body that was larger and deeper than most guitars, and was made with a solid Sitka spruce top, Brazilian rosewood back and sides (replaced by East Indian rosewood from 1969), ebony fingerboard, black-and-white binding and ornamentation with 5/16-inch non-scalloped braces.

The rest of the industry followed Martin's lead, and the Dreadnought is now considered one of the classic acoustic guitar shapes, ideal for use in a wide variety of musical genres.

As of 2005, Martin offered more than 180 different models, and the D-28 has been much imitated but never bettered. It is easily the most recognizable acoustic guitar ever made.

The Martin D-28 has been a classic for over three quarters of a century and construction has changed little. The internal bracing has been altered, the width of the neck has been reduced, the herringbone trim has disappeared, and the position markers have changed from snowflakes to dots.

improvised with his backing musicians. The lengthy instrumental "Glistening Glyndebourne" found him amplifying his acoustic with a pickup and applying echo to the signal to create a trademark sound.

The final ingredient was alternate tunings, which he started using during years of playing solo when "it made it much easier to get a big, warm sound." One that he learned from Dick Gaughan (C–F–C–C–G–D from bottom to top), became known as "violin tuning," as the violin is tuned in fifths. "Once you get the basic shapes down it's very simple and sounds very sweet...very sonorous."

His favorite Martin D-28 was one of two gifts from the manufacturer. "It is particularly lovely 'cos it's got Maltese crosses all over it in the purling, the headstock and the twiddly bits—the machine heads! On the bridge it has inlays of mother of pearl. It's a lovely guitar, sounds nice and sweet. I take both my Martins on tour."

Martyn's career failed to follow any consistent path. Indeed, after 1973's *Solid Air* had taken him to the edge of the mainstream (one track, "May You Never," attracting a cover by Eric Clapton), its jazz-rocky follow-up *Inside Out* returned him to cult status and a musician's musician. After battling ill-health and having his right leg amputated, Martyn died of double pneumonia in January 2009.

> **Notable Martin players:** Hank Williams; Elvis Presley, whose D-18 sold for $180,000 in the early 1990s; Jimi Hendrix, whose D-45 was allegedly his favorite guitar of all time.

MODULUS FLEA BASS
FLEA

The funk-metal formula of the Red Hot Chili Peppers saw them make a name for themselves in the 1980s. They cut their teeth on covers of black classics, like Stevie Wonder's "Higher Ground" and Hendrix's "Fire." But they spent significantly more time on crafting their own material as their career developed, and the backbone of the songs came from the groove-laden bass of Michael Balzary, aka Flea.

After fourteen years of struggle, the Chili Peppers hit a career peak in 1992 when the millionth *BloodSugarSexMagik* album was sold. The sound changed and, as they became more song based, they lost some old fans but gained millions of new ones. As time went by Flea moved from Stingray basses to the signature

Modulus Flea Bass. His one modification to the instrument, replacing the stock bridge with a Leo Quan Badass, was reflected in the production model in 1999, two years after its launch.

Flea took delivery of the first Silver Flake Flea Bass to be made but in 1999 it met a sorry end during a San Francisco gig when it was smashed to bits (the graphite neck proved impervious to damage and was recycled).

The Modulus Flea was used on the album *Californication* and when Flea guested with Jane's Addiction on *Kettle Whistle*.

In 2009, having cut ties with Modulus, he launched the affordable China-made Fleabass (one word), aimed at beginners and finished in a mouth-watering choice of colors. This is in no way related to the Modulus Flea and, unsurprisingly given the price, had a conventional (nongraphite) maple neck in either 30-inch (junior) or regular 34-inch scale.

Dave Ellefson, once of Megadeth, has used the Modulus Flea Bass, though it's likely professional players have shied away from endorsing someone else's signature model.

MODULUS FLEA BASS

Guitar maker Rick Turner is credited with making the first graphite neck for a bass guitar while at Alembic in 1977. Together with San Franciscan bassist and aerospace designer Geoff Gould he subsequently set up the Modulus Graphite Company to explore the possibilities of the material. The advantages of graphite, a carbon composite previously used on NASA space probes, included the elimination of dead spots on the neck, ensuring the strings gave an even response across the board, while clarity and sustain were also improved.

Products included the Quantum and Genesis basses. But it was the Flea Bass (designed in conjunction with Flea) that put the company on the map in 1997. It had a uniquely shaped double-cutaway alder body, but it was the carbon fiber neck with its compound-radius composite fingerboard, pearl-dot position markers, and bidirectional relief-adjusting rod that was the attraction.

It was said by *Bassist* magazine that you could put the neck between two chairs and stand on it without damaging it, while another impressed critic claimed: "I can't believe that a neck can be so even, flat and perfect. No dead spots (or hot spots), no problems with frets raising, etc. The carbon fiber gives you a level of perfection that simply isn't possible with wood."

The Modulus Quantum bass neck featured on these basses was a lightweight, ultra-rigid D-shaped shell made from dozens of layers of hand-formed, aerospace-grade, epoxy-impregnated carbon fibers. The Basslines MM (MusicMan-style) pickup was controlled by a Bartolini active tone system with master volume and two-band EQ. In the summer of 2008 the Modulus Flea bass became the Funk Unlimited bass when artist and manufacturer ended their association.

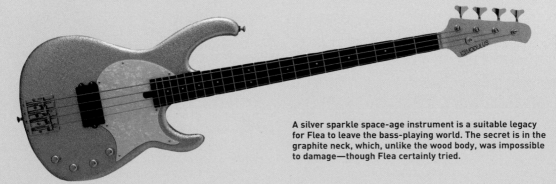

A silver sparkle space-age instrument is a suitable legacy for Flea to leave the bass-playing world. The secret is in the graphite neck, which, unlike the wood body, was impossible to damage—though Flea certainly tried.

MOSRITE
JOHNNY RAMONE

Guitarist Johnny Ramone was in at the birth of punk at legendary New York club CBGBs in 1974. The Ramones' first tour of the U.K. two years later, playing short, sharp, pointed, and often humorous songs, influenced the first wave of U.K. punk bands.

Johnny, born John Cummings, chose a Mosrite, a guitar he once said was "made of really good cardboard," as his instrument because, "I wanted a guitar no one else was using, something to be identified with. It was lightweight, with a sound of its own and a neck thin enough to play barre chords. My first one

cost fifty dollars from [famous Forty-eighth Street New York music store] Manny's."

Ramone's super-functional Ventures II Mosrite, with its single volume and tone controls, became the iconic punk guitar. Its buzz-saw sound was apparent on the band's first three albums, *Ramones*, *Leave Home*, and *Rocket to Russia*, issued between 1976 and 1977. He had deliberately limited musical ambitions: "A lot of guitar players play certain things I wish I could play, but I never really worked at it hard enough. I never wanted to be in this band or that band. The Ramones

MOSRITE

Mosrite guitars were the brainchild of Semie Moseley and manufactured in Bakersfield, California, from the late 1950s to the 1990s, with a gap in the middle from 1969 to 1984. A minister friend, the Reverend Ray Boatright, put up the money for the company, which combined the pair's last names, in 1952.

Their first spell of popularity was with surf bands and particularly instrumental band the Ventures, whose popularity in Japan made the brand legendary there. They were noted for their very thin, low-fretted (sometimes called "speed frets"), and narrow necks, while many bodies exhibited a "German Carve" on the top that Moseley learned from Roger Rossmeisl while learning his trade at Rickenbacker. A recognition feature is the outline of the letter "M" cut in the top of the headstock.

The archetypal Mosrite guitar's body shape was curiously bottom-heavy when compared with a Fender; indeed, it resembled a "reversed Stratocaster," but this was part of its gawky charm. Typically two P-90-style pickups were fitted, both governed by single tone and volume knobs;

these were selected via a toggle switch, and the neck one was set at a pronounced diagonal angle to the strings. Some had hand vibrato units designed by Moseley himself. This was the Vibramute, and it consisted of a solid cast-metal base and a string stop connected to a vibrato arm, which was lifted by a large spring.

At the peak of production in 1968, Semie, his brother Andy, and their 107 employees were making about 1,000 guitars a month. Mosrite's production line shifted to Japan—the country where the marque's following was always strongest—in 1992.

The design has attracted many homages, notably from Australian makers Wilson Brothers and Tym Guitars. Indeed, there have been more copies of Mosrites made than the genuine article, including many fakes.

This (right) is an Eastwood copy of Johnny Ramone's Mosrite guitar. Known as the JR Elite, it is correct to the last detail, including the mismatched knobs.

is loud, exciting rock 'n' roll and I don't think anybody can really top what we do."

His original instrument was stolen in 1977 along with some other band equipment. It was replaced by a white Mosrite to which a stop tailpiece and heavy-duty Grover machine heads were added. He invariably favored the bridge pickup with more treble, and some of his guitars having the more mellow neck unit disconnected entirely.

The Ramones bowed out in early 1996 and Johnny died in September 2004, just four days after a tribute concert at the Avalon in Hollywood to celebrate the band's thirtieth anniversary.

Notable Mosrite players: Fred Sonic Smith (MC5); Kurt Cobain; Nokie Edwards (the Ventures); Keith Smith (B-52s).

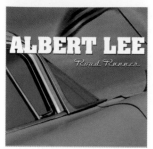

MUSICMAN GUITAR
ALBERT LEE

Albert Lee is a well-respected British guitarist who made his name in the United States. He based himself there after the early 1970s breakup of his British band, Heads Hands and Feet. He has since played with such high-profile acts as the Everly Brothers, the Crickets, and Emmylou Harris. He also spent several years in the 1980s as Eric Clapton's onstage foil.

His mainstays were always the Telecaster and, less frequently, the Stratocaster, but he started working closely with MusicMan in the mid-1980s, and their instruments have benefited from his expertise. "In (my early) days I swapped around a lot and it's only in the last thirty years I've settled on one guitar with my MusicMan."

In the mid-1980s the Silhouette six string was the first new design to emerge from MusicMan after its acquisition by string makers Ernie Ball. The Fender-inspired guitar was designed by Dudley Gimpel, with input from Lee. "The pickup setup on that is very

much the same as the Strat—three pickups, five-way switch, volume and tone. It's for me an ideal combination."

The body is smaller and sustains a little more than a Strat, while the pickups are by Seymour Duncan. "Seymour's been a good friend over the years; he knew the sound I like—vintage-style pickups. In a way it's like a vintage Strat except the back pickup is more like a Tele; it's got a metal plate under it and it's got a bit more volume than a Strat pickup would have."

Lee met Leo Fender a couple of times when he was involved in MusicMan, and he has a theory why the single coil became the sound of country music. "I never asked him but I think he had a hearing problem where he couldn't hear the highs too well, so he made his guitars really bright. I heard that story a long time ago, that he liked that bright sound. I still like that sound. It cuts through." Lee teamed his guitar with MusicMan amps until reverting to Fender amplification.

Notable MusicMan players: Steve Morse (Dixie Dregs, Deep Purple), Steve Lukather (Toto) and Eddie Van Halen have been numbered among MusicMan six stringers. Silhouettes similar to Lee's have been toted by Rolling Stones Ronnie Wood and Keith Richards.

MUSICMAN GUITAR

Leo Fender left the company that bears his name in 1965, and he was forbidden by the terms of the agreement to re-enter the music-instrument business for a decade. MusicMan was set up in 1972 by ex-employee Tom Walker and Forrest White, and he joined them when he could. The Stingray bass was their most successful product, but the Silhouette, introduced in 1986 after the Ernie Ball takeover, reinterpreted Leo's Stratocaster in a more modern way.

It would capture the imagination of a number of leading players who would use it as the basis for their own signature models. The Albert Lee Silhouette is marketed under the slogan "All the snap and pop of a Tele-style guitar, with the versatility of a Stratocaster." It is notably more angular than many MusicMan guitars and has a distinctive trapezoidal scratchplate. Its Southern ash body is teamed with a fast maple neck and fingerboard, the 25.5-inch scale length and 1.6-inch neck width at the nut, making for a comfortable feel. Three Seymour Duncan Custom pickups capture Lee's sound and are assisted by a so-called tone block or piece of mahogany that "filters" the bright tones and adds a final touch of warmth.

Other features include a hardened-steel bridge with string-through-body capability, while a special five-bolt joint links body and two-octave twenty-four-fret maple neck. The headstock is the distinctive four and two split of tuners favored by MusicMan six-string guitars, which echoes the Stingray bass.

The MusicMan six stringer (left), with humbucking pickups and rosewood fretboard and Albert Lee's signature writ large on the headstock.

MUSICMAN STINGRAY BASS
JOHN DEACON

Born in 1951, John Deacon was the youngest Queen member, as well as the last to join. In a group where Freddie Mercury, Brian May, and Roger Taylor vied for the spotlight, he was the quiet one. "But I think I fitted in because of that. They'd tried several other bass players before me, but their personalities seemed to clash."

His main fretted basses were two late-1960s Fender Precisions; both were originally sunburst, but he stripped them back to bare wood. One was refinished in black and became his main instrument, with the other as backup. In 1975 guitarist May challenged him to use a double bass on his song "39." Deacon rose to the task, and a couple of days later he was found in the studio with the instrument, which he had already learned to play adequately. He acquired a fretless Precision in 1977, which he

MUSICMAN STINGRAY BASS

MusicMan guitars' first production model, the Stingray, was considerably more successful in its four-stringed variant than the accompanying guitar. It is now running a close third to Fender's Precision and Jazz as popular music's definitive four-string bass. Its "honky" tone, derived from a single large humbucking pickup, cut through the mix, while its asymmetric headstock configuration with three tuners above and one below, was equally visually distinctive. Other recognition features included an egg-shaped pickguard and a three-knob silver control plate. It came with a choice of maple or rosewood fingerboard and had a smooth satin-finish back to its neck, which players either loved or hated.

The Stingray was the first production bass to feature active electronics in a treble- and bass-boost facility; most guitars simply rolled off the treble or bass tone. Active midboost was a later option; this system was known as 3EQ and necessitated an extra knob. (No bass had offered this kind of versatility before without the aid of an expensive onboard preamp.) The result was a classic that proved particularly popular with disco and funk artists.

String manufacturer Ernie Ball took over MusicMan in the mid-1980s and moved them to a new plant in San Luis Obispo, California, in 1985. Leo Fender himself had already bailed out to form G&L with old colleague George Fullerton.

The five-string Stingray 5 emerged in 1987 and featured a three-way toggle switch that allowed the player to split the humbucking pickup's coils. In 2005, two-pickup versions of the Stingray (known as HH and HS) were introduced, with a five-way switch allowing the user not only to split coils but to select different combinations of humbucker and single-coil pickups. This greatly increased the diversity of available tones.

The humbucking pickup of the MusicMan Stingray (left) was ideal for funk-based music. Its massive output was controlled by an active EQ affecting treble, mid, bass, and volume.

would use solely for that number onstage and, later, "My Melancholy Blues."

It was around 1980 that he acquired a MusicMan Stingray, and songs like "Dragon Attack" and "Another One Bites the Dust" feature this bass prominently. He was the only member to favor this style. In "Another One Bites the Dust" he wrote the chart-topping number that established Queen in the United States in 1980. That distinctive bass line, which could only have been played by a Stingray, owed a debt to Chic's "Good Times," suggesting his purchase of the instrument was in emulation of Bernard Edwards.

Deacon was a notable absentee from the Queen + Paul Rodgers reunion project and the group's 2001 induction into the Rock & Roll Hall of Fame, and he appears to have retired from active music making, firm in the belief that the death of Freddie Mercury in 1991 effectively ended the group. His Stingray is now on display at the Hard Rock Cafe in Cleveland, Ohio.

Notable Stingray players: Cliff Williams (AC/DC); Flea (Red Hot Chili Peppers); Tony Levin (for Peter Gabriel).

NATIONAL AIRLINE GUITAR
JACK WHITE

Born John Anthony Gillis in 1975, Jack White came to fame as frontman of alt-rock duo White Stripes, but he has diversified to play in several bands, including the Raconteurs.

The guitars he uses live tend toward retro sounds and styles. Chief among the former are two 1965 Res-O-Glass Airlines (one which he received from a fan), a Kay Hollowbody, a Crestwood Astral II, and a Harmony Rocket. The angular, red Airline is commonly referred to as the JB Hutto model, named after a legendary bluesman and slide guitarist.

There's more to Jack White's art than

simply buying up old guitars and amps. "I don't want people to think that the gear is all it takes to get my sound," White explains. "I also didn't want people to think I'm precious or retro simply because I don't use brand-new equipment."

At the heart of that sound is his Airline. "Playing that guitar makes me feel like I have to take something that's broken and make it work," he says. "It's hollow, it's made of plastic, and it feels like it's going to fall apart. The front pickup is broken, but the treble pickup has an amazing bite. I've never had it refretted or anything. It's pretty much the way I found it, except for new tuners."

The effects he uses include Digitech Whammy, Electro Harmonix Pog (polyphonic octave generator), and Electro-Harmonix Big Muff distortion/sustain pedal, running simultaneously into a Fender Twin Reverb and a 100-watt Silvertone 6-by-10-inch combo. In both cases, White's guitar tone is the sound of gear in the signal chain being pushed to its limit. "I don't know what makes an amp work, but I...pay a lot of attention to making my tone as powerful as it can be."

That tone can be heard at its most primal on 2003's "Seven Nation Army," one of the most instantly recognizable guitar riffs of the past decade. It was played on an Airline through the EHX octave pedal. The opening track on the White Stripes' fourth studio album, *Elephant*, was also the LP's first single, hitting Number 7 in the U.K. and topping the Modern Rock Chart in the United States.

NATIONAL AIRLINE GUITAR

The National name first appeared on guitars in the late 1920s, and it is synonymous with retro designs. They were also responsible for the striking resonator guitar. The Valco company made instruments under its flagship National brand and its budget Supro guitar brand. Their "airline map" guitars with fiberglass bodies were given the name because they looked superficially like a map of the United States. These guitars were made in the U.S. between 1958 and 1964 and sold through the Montgomery Ward mail-order retail company. The Valco company went out of business in 1968.

The Airline Town & Country Guitar combined the design features of the Airline with a slightly larger body and a 1960s pickguard, while a Barney Kessel signature model, made for the celebrated jazz musician, was marketed to the public as the Tuxedo.

The mere shape of the National guitar is enough to evoke nostalgia, even if many players had no idea what most of the controls were meant to do. While original Nationals had fiberglass bodies, later replicas have tended to favor more conventional wood construction. Recently these have been made by Robin Guitars in Texas, while a small factory in San Luis Obispo, California, has produced more than 15,000 instruments in nearly two decades under the name National Reso-Phonic Guitars Inc.

The JB Hutto Airline model has been reissued by Eastwood Guitars in the early 2000s under the name of the Airline DLX with many noticeable structural and aesthetic differences. Most notably, Eastwood guitars are built in China using chambered mahogany bodies as opposed to the hollow fiberglass (or "Res-O-Glas") bodies used for the originals.

The guitar at the right is one of the more elaborate Airline guitars with three pickups and double the number of switches to control them. Nevertheless, the resulting sound is pleasingly primitive.

NATIONAL STYLE O RESONATOR
MARK KNOPFLER

Dire Straits' *Brothers in Arms* was promoted by CD pioneers Philips as a technological masterpiece in an attempt to popularize the then-new digital sound carrier. Yet its cover featured a very traditional instrument. The album sold more than 22 million copies and spent 200 weeks on the British chart. Mark Knopfler wrote the songs, sang them, and supplied the guitar hooks.

The album's cover features a National Style O Resonator guitar engraved with palm trees; Knopfler bought it from friend Steve Phillips for £120. The photo was taken on the island of Montserrat where recording was taking place; New York photographer Debbie Feingold flew in to do the job. "It doesn't have any significance," says Knopfler, "except that the guitar's very special to me because I learned a lot of my music on that style of instrument."

In the United States, *Brothers in Arms* slipped into pole position on the last day of August 1985, holding onto the Number 1 spot for nine weeks. Britain had seen it hit the top three months earlier, its fortnight stay followed by a similar spell in August. The album displaced Bruce Springsteen's *Born in the USA*—a thrill for Knopfler, who was born just six weeks before the Boss.

The resonator guitar has been used on keynote Dire Straits tracks "Romeo and Juliet," "Telegraph Road" (with its stirringly evocative introduction), and, from *Brothers in Arms*, "The Man's Too Strong." And it saw even greater use when Knopfler got together with friends Steve Phillips and Brendan Croker in 1990 to play the clubs as the acoustic-based Notting Hillbillies.

There are two major brand names of resonator guitar: National and Dobro. Knopfler favored the National sound made famous by players such as Son House, Rory Gallagher, and Keb' Mo', while Dobro aficionados included Eric Clapton and Jerry Douglas.

NATIONAL STYLE O RESONATOR

A resonator, or resophonic, guitar is an acoustic guitar in which one or more metal cones, or resonators, make the sound instead of the wooden soundboard of a conventional instrument. Resonator guitars were designed to compete with the horns and percussion instruments of dance orchestras. They soon became valued for their distinctive sound, especially in the fields of bluegrass and blues; this continued long after electric amplification solved the issue of inadequate guitar sound levels.

Resonator guitars are built in the style of National or Dobro, the two companies that invented, designed, and built resonator guitars in the 1920s and 1930s. The main difference between the two is the design of the resonator cones. Nationals use two systems: the Tricone, which utilizes three 6-inch resonators and the single cone, which is larger at 9.5 inches. The pressure of the strings running across the bridge pushes down on the cones and amplifies the sound.

The Dobro's resonator cone is upside down by comparison, and the bridge assembly (known as the spider) transmits the sound to the edge of the cone rather than to the center, as is the case with Nationals. These two contrasting systems create very different tonal qualities. Most blues, Hawaiian, rock, and jazz players prefer National guitars, while country and folk players prefer Dobros. The second half of the 1980s and early 1990s saw National-style guitars produced by a new wave of makers in the U.K. A variety of quality budget-price instruments is now available from AMG, Ozark, and others.

The National Style O Resonator (left) was introduced in 1930 and was available until 1941. The manufacturer incorporated a variety of design scenes, with palm trees, clouds, and stars adorning the front, back, and sides.

OVATION BALLADEER
JOAN ARMATRADING

St. Kitts–born, Birmingham-raised singer-songwriter Joan Armatrading shot to world fame with the 1976 album that took her name and contained the smash hit "Love and Affection." By the millennium she'd chalked up fifteen studios albums (plus compilations and a live effort), worked with the cream of the world's musicians, and won a coveted Ivor Novello Award in 1996 for her career achievements. Not bad for a musician whose first guitar had been obtained by her mother in exchange for two old baby strollers!

While she entered the electric arena late, notably with 2007's *Into the Blues*, Armatrading's strong, rhythmic acoustic-guitar playing was a trademark of her early work. She settled upon the Ovation Balladeer in 1973 after becoming frustrated in the hunt for an acoustic Martin, Guild, or Gibson. A sales assistant in a London music store brought her the instrument after she'd tried and rejected dozens. What

OVATION BALLADEER

The Ovation company was owned by helicopter manufacturer Charles Kaman, himself a guitar player, and founded in Connecticut in 1966. They used synthetic materials as well as wood to make their revolutionary instruments. The idea was to use Lyracord (their trade name for fiberglass) to avoid problems associated with the instability of wood. While their solid-bodied electric guitars and basses proved briefly popular with the likes of Steve Marriott and Jeff Lynn's ELO, Ovation's biggest contribution to the music world was making the electro-acoustic guitar a reality for thousands of musicians.

The Ovation line typically had a "bowl back," which was thinner yet stronger than its wood equivalent. Furthermore, it was suggested that this "parabolic bowl" efficiently gathered the sound waves and focused them through the sound hole.

Another big advance was the use of piezotransducer pickups, one under each individual string saddle and buried in the instrument's bridge. They proved far more effective and less likely to feed back than stick-on bugs, and the level of signal available to be output was incomparable. Some solid-body guitars today combine piezo pickups and conventional pickups.

The Balladeer was one of the first Ovation models, alongside the Classic and Josh White. The Adamas range of Ovations that succeeded the Balladeer in 1976 had multiple sound holes, a complicated construction facilitated by the use of carbon graphite in the actual top of the guitar. Kaman re-entered the solid-body market by buying Hamer in 1988, but they will always be known first and foremost for electro-acoustics.

The distinctive Ovation headstock is a recognition feature, but the revolutionary features of this acoustic guitar (left)— its piezo pickup and non-wood "bowl back"—are not visible in this shot.

caught her ear was the fact that "it projects the sound well and is a true reproduction of an acoustic sound, which is the main thing." She also marveled at its lack of feedback and the fact she could literally "plug in and play."

She used to play Yamaha acoustics but "can't go back to the box shape. I like the sound of the other guitars, but when I'm standing up it's too awkward....I really liked the Ovation, and I've been using it ever since. I think I got my first twelve string in 1973 or 1974 as well."

Armatrading has since gone on to endorse further Ovation models, including the Legend, a twelve string, and a mandolin. The *Steppin' Out: Live!* album from 1979 showcases her playing on Ovation acoustics on tracks like "Cool Blue Stole My Heart." Armatrading plays all of her instruments through a custom sound system made by Pete Cornish; she commissioned him after having been impressed by Mark Knopfler's similar system.

Notable Ovation players: Jazz musician Charlie Byrd; Glen Campbell; Richie Sambora; Melissa Etheridge.

PAUL REED SMITH (PRS)
CARLOS SANTANA

Carlos Santana's classic early recordings were made with a standard Gibson SG, but he was never happy with it because "it went out of tune too much…and I need all the help I can get." Yamaha stepped into the breach, and from the 1970s he was to be seen playing an SG2000. A vintage Les Paul, which

PAUL REED SMITH

Paul Reed Smith has always made guitars without compromise. He knew he needed to raise heavyweight finance to set up production, so he took two prototypes on the road. Only when he had $300,000 worth of orders did he raise $500,000 to build a factory. This ensured that, for many years, demand exceeded supply.

He sought to embody the classic Les Paul virtues when creating the PRS Custom in 1985, though he cleverly nodded to the Strat with a double cutaway and a five-way pickup option allowing the PRS-manufactured humbuckers to offer both humbucking and single-coil sounds. The instrument weighs significantly less than the Les Paul at 8 pounds, while the double cutaway offers better top-fret access.

Two decades later, Smith and Santana teamed up to design, build, and sell the PRS Santana model guitars. The main models are taken from exactly what Santana plays, and he sometimes uses production models onstage and in the studio. As his desired features have

changed, so the guitars have been modified over time: this has resulted in Santana I, Santana II, Santana III, and Santana MD models.

The PRS models are mahogany with maple tops, and often they are exquisitely flamed. Distinctive bird-shaped mother-of-pearl inlays decorate the fretboards of his top-level guitars, the lower-spec instruments making do with crescent-shaped inlays. With hollowed-out chambers in their body, PRS guitars have the ability to provide some of the fat tone of a Gibson Les Paul without the Les Paul's spine-crushing weight. Smith has never bought into the concept of "vintage" pickups, believing the sound comes from woods and construction.

SE (Student Edition) PRSs have been made in the Far East and appear to have found a ready market without devaluing the premium brand.

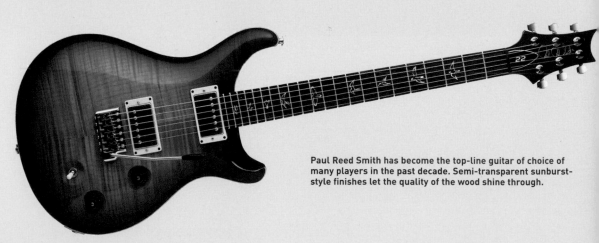

Paul Reed Smith has become the top-line guitar of choice of many players in the past decade. Semi-transparent sunburst-style finishes let the quality of the wood shine through.

he had purchased early in the decade, also remained a part of his armory.

But it was Baltimore-based guitar maker Paul Reed Smith with whose products he is now irrevocably associated. Smith made his first instrument for Santana four years after getting backstage with a prototype instrument in 1976.

It cleverly combined the double-cutaway body style that Carlos favored with a 24.5-inch scale length that was close enough to Gibson's (25-inch) for it to feel familiar to playing SG and Les Paul guitars. The twenty-four frets also allowed Santana to play a high E without bending, particularly useful as many of his songs are in the key of E and A.

The solid construction of the guitar offered the sustain that has been his trademark since hits from the early 1970s like "Evil Ways," "Oye Como Va," and "Black Magic Woman." He typically holds notes through chord and tempo changes before breaking off into sparkling clusters of notes and repetitive riffs. He rarely uses effects, preferring to plug in and make the guitar sing. He has praised the PRS for helping him "finally get into those low John Coltrane notes," and said "with some guitars you just get green and yellow—this is like the full rainbow."

Santana played his PRS on the 1999 Number 1 single "Smooth"—his first U.S. Top 40 hit since 1982 and his first chart topper ever. "Since I played that guitar I can't go back to anything else," he said. He did, however, warn prospective purchasers that "I can tell you every piece of gear I've ever used and you're still not going to sound like me."

Notable Paul Reed Smith players: Alex Lifeson (Rush); Mark Tremonti (Creed); up-and-coming British bluesman Davy Knowles.

RED SPECIAL
BRIAN MAY

Thanks to the huge success of his group Queen, Brian May ended the 1970s as one of rock's highest profile guitarists. He was also the man with the most distinctive guitar sound to his name, partly due to the homemade Red Special he'd made with the help of his father, Harold.

But May hadn't planned on rock stardom, believing his future lay in astrophysics; and in 1967 he was accepted to study at London's Imperial College. He kept his hand in with some part-time guitar playing, until linking with Roger Taylor in what was to become the band Queen. Around 1964, unable to afford the Fender Stratocaster hanging in his local music shop, the young May set about building the guitar that would play such a crucial role in the distinctive Queen sound. Brian carved the neck by hand from a piece of 100-year-old mahogany fireplace, and the core of the body from ancient oak. The name "Red Special" came from the red/brown color of the guitar after it was stained, and painted with numerous layers of Rustin's plastic

RED SPECIAL

The Red Special guitar, in tune with Brian May's own playing style, features a thick neck. It has a 24-fret oak fingerboard, and position inlays hand-shaped from mother-of-pearl buttons and placed in original, helpful patterns. The strings pass over a zero fret and through a Bakelite string guide. Originally the guitar had a built-in distortion circuit, adapted from a mid-1960s Vox distortion unit, but this was removed when May discovered that he preferred the unique compression sound of a treble boost pedal through a Vox AC30 at full volume.

In the 1990s, Greg Fryer spent two years making three meticulous replicas of the Red Special, two of which have accompanied Brian on tour ever since. Commercial replicas have been manufactured during the 1980s and 1990s by the Guild Guitar Company from 1983 to 1991 and by Burns Guitars in the late nineties. In the twenty-first century, through the new 'Brian May Guitars' company, Brian took control of the manufacture himself, and in addition to the mass-produced Specials, employed KZ GuitarWorks in Japan to make a super high quality hand-finished instrument which became known the 'Super.' The ultimate copies available commercially are hand-made to the exact Red Special specs by master luthier Andrew Guyton in Norfolk, England.

In 2006, Brian May Guitars introduced a scaled-down Red Special or "Mini May" with a single pickup, no switches and a maple neck. An acoustic guitar featuring a twenty-four-fret neck and the body outline of the Red Special went into production in 2007.

Today Brian continues to experiment with sounds and techniques, and the reputation of Brian May Guitars now holds its own alongside the best in guitar shops around the world. The original Red Special still appears with Brian whenever he plays on stage. He says it will just about see him out!

The distinctive silhouette of the Red Special.

coating. The tremolo arm was made from an old bicycle saddlebag carrier, the knob at the end of it from a knitting needle, and the springs for a self-designed tremolo were recycled from an old motorbike. Brian originally wound his own pickups but when they didn't perform satisfactorily under conditions of string-bending, he walked into the new Burns shop in Centre Point and purchased three Tri-Sonic pickups at three guineas each, which, fitted to the Red Special, became part of the distinctive Brian May sound.

Brian's guitar was quickly put to use in his first pop combo, 1984, a semi-pro outfit based in Hampton Grammar School. As if such a unique guitar wasn't enough, May did things differently at the plucking end. "I use an English sixpence instead of a plectrum because it's not flexible . . . you get more control if all the flexing is felt in the fingers. You have total control . . . and by holding it at different angles you can get different attack effects on the notes, from a smooth hit, to an articulated rasp, especially when you're using the guitar at high volume, as I generally do."

The Red Special has featured on every Queen album recorded, on chart-topping tracks like "Bohemian Rhapsody" and "Under Pressure," and in every one of the band's gigs—a tribute to both the guitar and its maker.

At the end of the Queen + Paul Rodgers tour in 2005, May had the zero fret replaced and made a larger opening for a new output jack. Astonishingly, the rest of the original frets on the guitar have never been replaced.

Replica Red Specials are used every night by guitarists at the Queen musical *We Will Rock You*, staged in London's West End from 2002 and subsequently worldwide, notably in Italy, Germany, Russia, Japan, Australia, South Africa, and Las Vegas. They are, of course, an essential purchase for any Queen tribute band.

RICKENBACKER 345 and 360/12
PETE TOWNSHEND

The driving force of the Who since their inception in the early 1960s, Pete Townshend has always been famed for his destruction of guitars. Yet the habit began by accident at the Railway Tavern, Harrow, in September 1964. He banged a Rickenbacker 1998 (an export version of the 345) on the ceiling of the venue. "The neck broke off because Rickenbackers are made out of cardboard. I had no recourse but to make it look like I had meant to do it. So I smashed this guitar and jumped all over the bits. Then I picked up the twelve string and carried on as though nothing had happened.

The next day the place was packed." The 1998 in question was the guitar pictured in the famous "Maximum R&B" Marquee Club poster. Townshend is reckoned to have destroyed nearly 100 guitars at gigs between 1964 and 1973, including eight Rickenbackers. He would repair destroyed ones for further stage use. "I was perversely proud of the fact that I was smashing up the most expensive guitar in London shops during the early 1960s when I still didn't own a car or an apartment."

Rickenbackers ("Rickies" for short) were popular with British Invasion bands like the

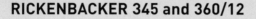

RICKENBACKER 345 and 360/12

The Rickenbacker guitar as we know it began life in 1958 as the creation of German designer Roger Rossmeisl. The semihollow guitar body was a block of wood hollowed out from the rear, while the low-output "toaster-top" pickups (so named because of their split-chrome appearance) gave the guitar their distinctive jangle and chime. They were phased out between 1969 and 1970 and replaced by Hi-Gain pickups, which had twice the output of their predecessors but half as much charm. Many Rickenbacker guitars had distinctive tailpieces incorporating a capital R, while "cooker" control knobs with diamond-shaped pointers on top were another distinguishing feature.

In 1964 Rickenbacker introduced three twelve-string variations on their designs, and these became particularly popular after Beatle movie A Hard Day's Night of the same year, which featured George Harrison using the instrument. When Roger Rossmeisl left to go to Fender, his successor, Dick Burke, had devised a simple headstock arrangement for the twelve string in which the original six

tuners stayed where they were, the extra keys facing backwards at a 90-degree angle. This avoided the balance problems of an unsightly elongated head.

Instruments aimed at the British market had different designations; they could easily be identified by the fact that importers Rose Morris asked for them to be produced with "proper" f-holes rather than the "cat's eye" (slash-shaped) opening in the semihollow body that the standard domestic items possessed. Rose Morris also gave them different numbers, like the 1993 (360/12), 1996 (325), and 1998 (345).

As both the British invasion and the 1960s came to an end, Rickenbacker guitars fell out of fashion; however Rickenbacker basses remained in favor through the 1970s.

The most impressive thing about the Rickenbacker twelve string was its compact headstock. Note, too, the "cat's eye" hole in the body, denoting a U.S. model.

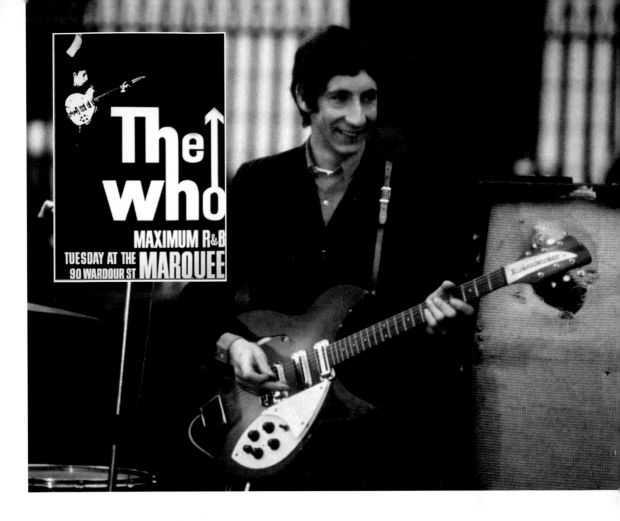

Beatles and the Who. Townshend not only used them onstage but also they were heard on early recordings, from "I Can't Explain," "Anyway, Anyhow, Anywhere" (both using a 1964 360/12 twelve string), and "My Generation" (the previously mentioned 1998 or 345) into the second LP, A Quick One.

Townshend continued to use Rickenbackers onstage and in the studio through 1965 and 1966, with a temporary switch, between December 1965 and January 1966, to a semihollow Grimshaw. He eventually began using solid-bodied guitars, like the Fender Telecaster or Stratocaster, for the destructive climax to the Who's stage act.

By early 1967, he was playing a new Rickenbacker Mapleglo 360/12 model, but by late 1968 had moved on to the Gibson SG. Townshend would later return to Rickenbackers in the studio, using a black 1964 330S/12 double-bound Fireglo twelve string extensively on the Face Dances LP in 1981 and, even later, on the solo Psychoderelict in 1993. Rickies reappeared in his stage act in 1980, then were used on the 1989 Who and 1993 solo Psychoderelict tour.

Rickenbacker launched the signature Pete Townshend Limited Edition in 1988, while "new Mods" the Jam paid tribute to the music of the era by using Rickenbackers throughout the 1970s.

Notable Rickenbacker 345 and 360/12 players: Paul Weller; Johnny Marr; Tom Petty; Serve Pizzorno (Kasabian); Roger McGuinn (the Byrds); Peter Buck (R.E.M.).

RICKENBACKER 360
PETER BUCK

R.E.M.'s guitarist and cofounder Peter Buck is the modern equivalent of the Band's Robbie Robertson: an anti-guitar hero. He rarely plays a superfluous note and solos just as infrequently; he simply serves the needs of the song with often deceptively simple guitar parts.

His guitar of choice is a black (Jetglo) Rickenbacker 360, which has been in almost

continuous use since the band's debut EP, *Chronic Town*, in 1982. It disappeared from the stage following a concert in Helsinki, Finland, in September 2008 but was happily returned intact nine days later. At this point Buck used five Rickies a night: a 330, 360/12, 620/12, and two 360/6 models.

His adoption of the brand had, he admits, been purely by chance. "When I first started playing I used to buy by color: what do you have in black guitars? They'd pull out five and I would pick one out. I was just lucky enough to stumble on a Rickenbacker.

"I've used my black 360 Rick on every record we've ever done. It's my main guitar; I bought it new, beat it up, splattered blood on it and now it's my guitar. You play a guitar for ten years and it's almost part of you." Amplification-wise he graduated from the Ampeg Gemini II used on the first album, *Murmur*, to Vox AC30s, then regressing to a small Silvertone.

Onstage the Rickenbacker remains a cornerstone of R.E.M.'s sound. In 2005, Buck revealed that of the twenty-four-song set played on their world tour, he employed one of several Rickenbackers on no fewer than seventeen of them.

> **Notable Rickenbacker 360 players:**
> Roger McGuinn of the Byrds obtained his "Mr. Tambourine Man" sound from a Rickenbacker twelve string.

RICKENBACKER 360

The Rickenbacker 360 guitar was pretty revolutionary when it appeared in the mid-1960s. Subtly updated through the years, this deluxe semihollow body remains visually and aurally unique today.

The body, developed from designer Roger Rossmeisl's Capri series of guitars of the late 1950s, is machined from a solid lump of maple (often two pieces joined at the center). The neck, made from three-ply maple/walnut, is set well into the body—all the way to the bridge pickup—and is stiffened by double truss rods, its thick rosewood fretboard finished with clear varnish.

Single-coil pickups isolated from the body by rubber grommets deliver everything from clean tone to biting overdrive. Controls include volume and tone via a three-way selector for each pickup, while a master preset allows tone and volume settings to be accessed instantly with a toggle. Stereo output is standard.

Rickenbacker began developing its electric twelve string in 1963, noting that the folk music revival of the early 1960s had seen a surge in popularity for the acoustic twelve string; the electric variety was then rare. The three-pickup 370/12 was favored by Roger McGuinn, while George Harrison retained his affection for the 360/12, calling it "the only twelve string you can change a string on when you're drunk."

The strings are in fact reversed in order—when strumming downward the bass strings are strummed first, which is against convention. But this enabled easier fretting and helped create the Rickenbacker's distinctive sound.

A beautiful Rickenbacker in Jetglo finish. The Ricky's distinctive jangle was popular in the 1960s and again in the 1980s, when the likes of the Smiths and R.E.M. brought it back.

RICKENBACKER BASS
CHRIS SQUIRE

Chris Squire started off playing Motown covers with the Syn in the mid-1960s before becoming a founding member of progressive rock legends Yes. "The fact that those [early Motown] songs had clever bass lines probably helped me develop as a player," he says.

The Syn made a Hendrix support appearance at London's Marquee Club in 1966. Amazingly, Squire played the Syn's reformation gig in 2005 with the same Rickenbacker 4001 he had played back then. "After I left school I spent a bit of time working in Boosey and Hawkes music store in Regent Street and they were the English agents for Rickenbacker," he explains, "so I managed to blag one at employee price! I've had it since about 1964."

Though he reckons it was the third to reach the U.K., other sources suggest Squire's Rickenbacker was actually the fourth to be imported after those for John Entwistle, the Kinks' Pete Quaife, and Donovan. Paul McCartney took his time to abandon his faithful Höfner violin bass and would also adopt a Rickenbacker, but not until later in the

decade. The dot fret markers, which McCartney's 4001S shares with Squire's instrument, identified it as an export model, as U.S. basses had triangular "shark's fin" inlays and fretboard binding.

Squire's bass playing is noted for being aggressive, dynamic, and melodic, and the Ricky's trebly cutting style suits this. He has also rewired his bass, enabling it to send a split signal to a conventional bass amplifier (the low-frequency output) and the high-frequency output to a separate lead guitar amplifier.

The instrument has appeared on every Yes album and can be heard effectively on signature tracks like "Roundabout" and "Yours Is No Disgrace." Even more

Rickenbacker can be heard on his 1975 solo debut, *Fish Out Of Water*.

He still uses his original Rickenbacker, which has been cloned by the manufacturers themselves and reissued as the limited edition 4001CS model.

Notable Rickenbacker bass players: It was Paul McCartney's regular post–*Sgt. Pepper* instrument, and many players such as Pink Floyd's Roger Waters and Rush's Geddy Lee investigated it thereafter. Motörhead's Lemmy is another notable user, as is the Stone Roses' "Mani" Mounfield.

RICKENBACKER BASS

Adolph Rickenbacker linked up with National guitars in 1931, but the company only started to enjoy success after Adolph sold out in 1953. The company's first bass, the 4000, appeared in 1957 and was followed by the 4001 in 1961. This would prove the most popular Ricky bass, and the basses in general would outstrip the company's six strings after the 1960s—Rickenbacker guitars were too associated with the beat boom to be "hip."

An unusual feature of the design is its two different pickups: the neck unit is a "toaster" and the brighter bridge a "horseshoe" pickup that wraps around the strings, rather than just sitting under them. The

combination makes the bass sound punchy yet full. Squire's pickup is underwound and he uses Rotosound roundwound strings for brightness. Many Rickenbacker players started off as guitarists and favor its toppy tone, sometimes described as "piano-like" and the antithesis of a Fender Precision, which has flat-wound strings and produces Motownesque sounds.

The 4001 bass has a neck-through-body construction using solid Eastern hard rock maple, a contoured body and Rickenbacker's famous chromed tailpiece-cum-bridge. The headstock has stuck-on "wings" of wood that mirror the body and give it a distinctive shape all its own.

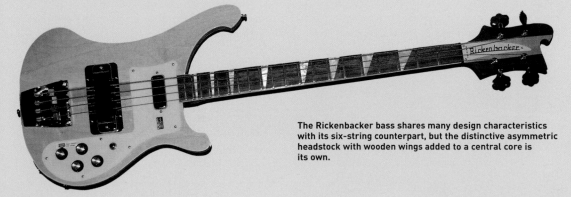

The Rickenbacker bass shares many design characteristics with its six-string counterpart, but the distinctive asymmetric headstock with wooden wings added to a central core is its own.

SELMER MODÈLE JAZZ
DJANGO REINHARDT

Django Reinhardt was one of the guitar's earliest champions, overcoming personal misfortune to conquer both Europe and the United States with his unique skills.

Born to a gypsy family in Belgium in 1910, he spent the majority of his youth around Paris. A neighbor gave the infant Reinhardt his first banjo-guitar, and he won a bet by playing seventeen melodies—which he'd heard played on an accordion just once—from memory and in the right order. By thirteen, Reinhardt had started playing in Parisian dance halls and was making his first recordings.

At eighteen he returned to his caravan and accidentally started a fire that transformed his home into an inferno. Reinhardt was left with a badly burned left hand, only two fingers retaining full mobility. His fourth and fifth digits had become permanently curled toward his palm, due to the tendons shrinking from the heat of the fire. Complete extension of these fingers was impossible, so he used them on the first two strings of the guitar for chords and octaves, leaving all soloing to be done with the index and middle fingers. Through adversity, Reinhardt had invented a technique that was entirely his own, and one that would

SELMER MODÈLE JAZZ

The Selmer guitar company made a wide variety of guitars, ranging from harp guitars through classical to Hawaiian, but the oval-hole Modèle Jazz is its best-known product. Early Selmers has a large, D-shaped sound hole (the *grande bouche*, or "big mouth"). This was shaped to accommodate an internal resonator, which was soon dropped.

Around 900 of Selmer's instruments produced between 1932 and 1952 were built in the Modèle Jazz style. Its back and sides were made of laminated Indian rosewood and a solid spruce top. Its walnut neck was a comparatively long, 26.5-inch scale with an ebony fingerboard, while a separate, grafted-on headstock had sealed tuners. These, the world's first sealed oil-bath machine heads, were the invention of Mario Maccaferri, designer of the original Selmer guitars (which are commonly known as Maccaferris).

Maccaferri had designed Selmer's original guitars, but his involvement with Selmer ended after eighteen months and, by 1936, the Modèle Jazz had appeared. Known as the *petite bouche* (small mouth) or "oval hole," the vast majority were sold in Selmer's native France.

While Maccaferri was no longer involved, the later guitars retained many unusual characteristics of his original innovative design, including a top that is bent, mandolin-style, behind the floating bridge—a factor that contributed to the guitar's remarkable volume when played.

The origin of the "small mouth" nickname is apparent in this view of the Selmer Modèle Jazz, on which so much of Django Reinhardt's music was made.

contribute significantly to the originality of his future compositions.

In 1934 a meeting with French violinist Stephane Grappelli spawned the legendary Quintette du Hot Club de France, one of the most original and influential bands in the history of recorded jazz. A succession of 78 rpm discs released on the Decca, Gramophone, Swing, and HMV labels included such legendary Reinhardt-Grappelli compositions as "Minor Swing" and "Black & White," as well as a string of jazz standards such as Cole Porter's "Night and Day." All featured his Selmer Modèle Jazz guitar.

Reinhardt had an endorsement deal with Selmer and was allowed to sell or give away guitars to friends or family. Thus many Modèle Jazz owners today believe theirs once belonged to Reinhardt. Of all the Selmers said to have been his, only two come with 100 percent proof of ownership.

Reinhardt continued to play, write, and record throughout the war years, somehow avoiding the fate of the Nazi concentration camps that befell many of his kinsfolk. A postwar U.S. tour with Duke Ellington expanded his horizons too, and by 1950 he was starting to experiment with amplification. It was a period that would spawn a number of acclaimed recordings, but it was ultimately cut short by the brain hemorrhage that caused his death in 1953.

STEINBERGER BASS
BILL WYMAN

Bill Wyman of the Rolling Stones celebrated his twentieth year as a professional musician by losing his head—his bass's head. Ned Steinberger's headless bass was the most eye-catching development since Ampeg/Dan Armstrong's experiments with Plexiglas a decade or so before, which had caught the eye of bandmate Keith Richards. As with Ford's Model T, the finish available was "any color as long as it was black."

The Steinberger player tuned the strings at the opposite end of the guitar from "conventional" instruments, and this could pose unexpected problems. When he took up the Steinberger in 1981, Wyman got over the problem of where to put his cigarette while playing by glueing the top of a ballpoint pen to the end of the neck.

Wyman's first bass was a Japanese instrument that he acquired while playing in R & B band the Cliftons in 1961. "Before that I'd been playing on the bottom two strings of a detuned guitar, so I was glad to finally have a 'real' bass. Unfortunately, it was bloody horrible!"

Interestingly, Wyman is credited with making the first-known fretless bass guitar in the early 1960s by converting an inexpensive Japanese fretted

STEINBERGER BASS

Ned Steinberger's headless bass, introduced in the early eighties, was made from graphite—hence there was no need for a weighty body. Neck and body were made from a one-piece molding, and innovative EMG active pickups were attached to the front of the guitar like a lid. The fretboard was also an added item; it was made of fiber-reinforced phenolic resin.

This wasn't by any means the first headless design in history—guitar pioneer Les Paul had experimented with them a decade or so before—while Modulus were already manufacturing bass necks from carbon graphite. But the way Steinberger, a nonmusician, married the concepts was breathtaking. The result was an instrument that looked different and sounded good, its clear, resonant tones likened by some to a piano.

A swiveling, detachable molding could be used to make the guitar balance when played sitting down, while a plastic extension attached to the strap sorted out matters standing up. Needless to say, the Steinberger's light weight made playing extended sets a joy.

There were remarks from less well-off players on the price of the instrument—around $2,000. But as Ned Steinberger himself explained in a 1988 magazine article, "it is fabricated from reinforced plastic, including as a major component carbon fiber one of the most expensive materials on the market, many times

the price of exotic hard wood." Add to that three years of research and it was evident why plastic, hitherto used on instruments to be sold cheaply, was out of the price range of many.

Steinberger would diversify and in some senses backtrack, making instruments with wooden bodies and even headstocks. But his L-2 in particular remains a bold design statement. Hohner were among the companies who marketed cheaper copies with wooden construction, so that those on a budget could adopt a touch of the Stones' style.

Tuning the Steinberger bass at the "wrong end" was just one of many challenges the headless bass posed to its users when introduced in the 1980s. Not least of which was where to stick your cigarette.

instrument. This can be heard on Rolling Stones songs such as "Paint it Black." Next stop was a semi-acoustic Framus Star Bass in 1964, due to its suitability for his small hands; then he moved on to a smaller Framus with an attractive striped wood-grain finish. The only Fender he was ever comfortable with was a short-scale Mustang.

After experimenting with a metal-necked Travis Bean, also an innovative guitar in its day, he adopted the Steinberger, using it on such albums as *Undercover* (1983), *Dirty Work* (1986), and *Steel Wheels* (1989), as well as in live performance. He continues to use it with his solo band, the Rhythm Kings.

Notable Steinberger players: Mike Rutherford (Genesis); Earl Falconer (UB40).

VOX TEARDROP
BRIAN JONES

Founding Rolling Stone guitarist Brian Jones used many guitars during his spell with the band. That tenure began in 1962 and ended just before his death in 1969. His main guitar in the early years, a Harmony Stratotone (sold at auction in London for £80,000 in June 2009), was replaced with a Gretsch Double Anniversary in two-tone green. From late 1965 until his death, Jones used various Gibsons (Firebirds, ES, and a Les Paul), as well as two Rickenbacker twelve strings. But there is surely no more iconic image of the band or the period than that of Jones performing onstage with his Vox Phantom Mark III (aka Teardrop).

Jones's customized specifications included having the headstock finished in white, making his instrument unique. Other modifications were two single pickups with the bridge unit right next to an early Fender Stratocaster bridge with pressed steel saddles, a tone and

volume knob for both pickups, and a three-way Fender-type pickup selector switch. He also changed the black scratch plate, preferring a chromed finish. This reflected lights back into the audience, drawing yet more attention to his guitar. Jones's guitar was made at the Dartford factory, not far from Jagger's and Richards's ancestral homes.

He used forms of open tuning, tuning the third string down, or sometimes adopting an open D. The teardrop can be heard on "The Last Time," a single they recorded at RCA Studios in Hollywood in 1965.

As the decade progressed, Keith Richards began to play more ambitious guitar parts while Jones, bored with the instrument, would find something exotic to play, though he was frequently absent from recordings as he became more and more detached from the group. Jones's only known guitar part from early 1966 until his death in 1969 was slide guitar on "No Expectations."

Fellow Stone Bill Wyman played a matching Vox bass for a time, and the semihollow teardrop Bill Wyman Signature Model was introduced in 1966. Various versions of the Vox Wyman bass were produced in both the U.K. and in Italy. A white Vox Teardrop guitar attributed to Jones could be seen at the Hard Rock Cafe in New York City in the eighties.

VOX TEARDROP

The Vox company was best known in the 1960s for its amplification, specifically the AC30 combo, but having tested the market with some budget equipment in 1959 they moved into the instrument market in 1961 with the angular Phantom. These featured metal pickup covers, a larger headstock, and a different vibrato than the guitars that would evolve in the Phantom series. The original is referred to as the Phantom Mark I, and it is estimated that only 150 were made.

Two years later came the third model in the Phantom series; it was appropriately named the Vox Phantom Mark III although, to this day, it is more commonly referred to as the Teardrop and was as aesthetically pleasing as the name suggests. Vox, who also made the Continental organ keyboard, then tried to market an organ/guitar hybrid, but this proved impractical. When demand exceeded supply, talks with Eko (another Italian company) took place, and Vox production at the Eko site in Recanati began in 1965. British-made Phantom and Teardrops have a higher collector value due to rarity, but they may be inferior to those made in Italy. Nevertheless, they are still treasured by fans and command high prices.

Because of bad business decisions, production of Vox guitars stopped in the U.K. by late 1967. Italian guitar production, which was controlled by Thomas Organ, continued until late 1969. Reproductions were put on the market after Vox's disappearance in 1969. These supposedly very British guitars of the 1960s were mainly made in Italy.

A modern replica of the Vox Teardrop, with Brian Jones's signature on the pickguard. The design's futuristic looks still impress nearly half a century on.

WARWICK BUZZARD
JOHN ENTWISTLE

John Entwistle, aka "the Ox," was the bass player of the Who from their formation in 1963 till his death in 2002. He played bass in the style of a lead instrument, resulting in a driving sound exemplified by his solo in 1965's "My Generation," achieved on a Fender Jazz.

Entwistle was a serious musician, having graduated from piano to play French horn in the Middlesex School's Orchestra. It proved a handy talent, too, as he performed and arranged all of the Who's studio brass arrangements until 1989. He'd later credit the combination of his school training on those various instruments for giving his fingers their impressive strength and dexterity.

He turned to bass with the Confederates before joining the Who, then known as the High Numbers. His first instrument, homemade through economic necessity, was

improvised by obtaining a piece of mahogany that was roughly the shape of a Fender body. He completed his handiwork on his grandmother's prized dining-room table and permanently damaged its surface.

In the midsixties, Entwistle was one of the first bassists to make use of Marshall stacks. He started using them in order to hear himself over Keith Moon's drums, so Pete Townshend then had to use them to be heard over Entwistle. He oscillated between Gibson, Fender, and Danelectro, while still retaining his trademark attacking style, but he ended up gravitating toward Alembic in the late 1970s and 1980s. (The Warwick Buzzard was used more for live performance than recording.)

By the time of his death he had amassed an impressive selection of instruments in his Cotswolds mansion; these were cataloged in a book, *Bass Culture: The John Entwistle Collection*. Sadly they had to be sold off by his family to pay death duties. Entwistle's collection of 150 guitars, thirty-three game fish, celebrity sketches, posters, and gold discs went under the hammer at Sotheby's in May 2003 and sold for a total of £1,093,372 ($1,761,798).

WARWICK BUZZARD

The graphite Buzzard John Entwistle toted in his latter Who days is rightly identified with him. He grew increasingly frustrated with tuning problems that Alembics encountered while playing outdoor concerts, due to the tendency of wood to expand or contract with changes in temperature and humidity. A battery problem at Live Aid in 1985 finally prompted him to create a bass made to his own specifications.

This was the Buzzard, whose angular, threatening appearance worked well with Entwistle's brooding stage presence. John approached Hans Peter Wilfer, founder of Warwick Basses, in 1985 and they came up with the Buzzard's unique design. Fewer than fifty were produced by Status Graphite before Entwistle's death. These have now become collector's items.

Status was the first company to build bass necks in carbon fiber rather than wood. Status had the patent for its use in basses and so they were commissioned to make the first Buzzards at Entwistle's request. The Status Buzzards feature a "basket-weave" pattern typical of carbon fiber. Although Warwick won the rights to continue the Buzzard name, they retained the body style of the Status original. Warwick produced about 100 Buzzards, but the playability and sound of the Status version is said to be superior.

The bass, which weighs a surprisingly light 7 pounds, is 55.5 inches long. Its widest point is 15.25 inches and, at the body's thickest area, it measures approximately 1.5 inches.

A few years after Entwistle's initial collaboration with Warwick, a graphite neck was introduced. Modulus Guitars provided bolt-on graphite necks for Warwick's wooden body. Warwick retained the licensing rights to produce Buzzard reissues after Hans Peter Wilfer proved in court that he had suggested eighty of the individual design details.

The unique profile of the Buzzard bass will forever be associated with its codesigner, John Entwistle. This example features two paired Fender Precision–style pickups.

YAMAHA SG1000
BOB MARLEY

Bob Marley, reggae's first and biggest global superstar, built on the pioneering work of Jimmy Cliff to break reggae music internationally, and Marley has proved irreplaceable since his death in 1981. He originally shared the spotlight in the Wailers with fellow vocalists Bunny Livingston and Peter "Tosh" McIntosh, but by the time Marley played the Lyceum in London in June 1975, he alone held center stage.

The cover of that breakthrough album, *Bob Marley and the Wailers Live!*, pictured him with a Gibson Les Paul guitar. By the time of his final worldwide tour in 1979, Marley was playing a Yamaha SG1000. In between the Les Paul and the Yamaha, Marley obtained a Washburn Hawk six string, which he gave to Canadian musician Gary Carlsen in November 1979.

He was presented with the SG1000 by the president of Yamaha when he and the Wailers were invited to visit the factory in Hamamatsu during the Tokyo leg of their tour.

Guitarists Junior Marvin and Al Anderson and bassist Aston Barrett were also given Yamaha instruments. (The Broad Bass was introduced in 1977 and quickly caught the attention of famous bass players throughout the world, including

YAMAHA SG1000

The Yamaha guitar has been around for more than sixty years and the company itself for more than a century. In 1965, it began production of solid-body guitars, mostly copies of U.S. designs, and by the 1970s its build quality had started to attract the attention of major artists, hence the decision to branch into original concepts.

The SG1000 and 2000 series was effectively a double-cutaway version of the Gibson Les Paul, which became successful in its own right. This was a high-quality guitar of original, if conservative, design that was the equal of the ubiquitous Strat and Les Paul. While the 1000 had a set neck, the 2000 had high-end neck-through-body construction, which gave excellent sustaining qualities. It also had a brass "sustain block" under the bridge and below the maple top.

The Yamahas had two humbucking pickups similar to the Les Paul, with a similar three-position pickup selector and a stop tailpiece. An innovation was coil taps operated by push-push switches (like a ballpoint pen), which allowed access to thinner single-pickup sounds. A carved maple top was applied to a mahogany body, whose double cutaway allowed access to the upper reaches of the twenty-two-fret ebony fretboard. Split fretboard inlays of mother-of-pearl/abalone were complemented by binding.

Yamaha exported to the U.S. (where they were known as the SBG series to avoid confusion with Gibson) until 1988. In 2007, Yamaha reissued the SBG2000 and SBG1000, both faithful reproductions of these two six-string classics. The limited edition SBG3000 then appeared in 2009 to celebrate forty years of exporting to the States.

Simple in design, the Yamaha SG1000 was Japan's answer to the Les Paul and became something of a modern classic.

Paul McCartney.) Barrett seems to have used his Yamaha BB up until the Gabon dates in the beginning of 1980; by the Uprising tour he was using his Fender Jazz again, while Marvin was pictured with his Yamaha at the Sunsplash 1979 festival.

Barrett says that Marley gave him the Yamaha after the Wailers' world tour in 1979, two years before he died. In 2000, Barrett allegedly gave it to a friend for "safe keeping" and was understandably shocked eight years later when he learned his prized possession was headed for auction; he sued his friend and the auction house for compensation and the guitar's return.

Notable Yamaha players: Al Di Meola; Steve Cropper; Phil Manzanera (Roxy Music); Paul Barrere (Little Feat); and Al McKay (Earth, Wind & Fire).

ZEMAITIS CUSTOM-BUILD
RONNIE WOOD

Ronnie Wood, who made his name playing bass for the Jeff Beck Group in the late sixties, switched to guitar when he joined the Faces at the turn of the decade.

He acquired his first Tony Zemaitis custom instrument in 1971 and refers to it as his "Stay with Me" guitar, as he was playing this when promoting the Faces' first hit single. The brand of boutique guitars has enjoyed the most

exalted patronage: apart from Wood and fellow Rolling Stone Keith Richards, other users have included Marc Bolan, Ronnie Lane and the Pretenders' James Honeyman Scott.

Wood has owned at least four metal-front Zemaitis guitars—three were stolen during tours in the seventies. One of these was maroon with an inlaid pearl dragon and was in the Les Paul–derived style that Zemaitis favored. The "Stay with Me" instrument is atypical in that respect, as well as in having push-button pickup selectors and three pickups instead of the usual two.

The outline of the guitar is Telecaster-like in shape, with a black mahogany body on which was inlaid a disc-shaped engraved metal panel typical of Zemaitis's handiwork. It is equipped with three closely spaced Gibson PAF pickups and has a twenty-four-fret fretboard. Wood

had insisted that his disc front have a bolt-on neck. Zemaitis explained that he didn't do bolt-on necks, but Wood was adamant. So Tony built a glued-neck disc front and simply screwed a neck plate on it in the appropriate place. The screws do not go through the body at all—it looks like a bolt-on, but isn't.

The Zemaitis was used extensively on Faces albums such as *A Nod's as Good as a Wink to a Blind Horse* (1971) and *Ooh La La* (1973), plus his own solo debut, *I've Got My Own Album to Do* (1974), tuning it to open E to facilitate slide playing.

After joining the Rolling Stones in 1975, Wood devised a unique way of combating theft of his guitars. A Zemaitis collector in Switzerland was invited to tour the world with the Stones in 1981 "as long as you bring your guitars with you."

ZEMAITIS CUSTOM-BUILD

The late Tony Zemaitis built his famous brand of handmade guitars in Kent from 1965 to 2000. A cabinet maker of Lithuanian heritage, his client list reads like a who's who of British rock. One of his acoustic guitars, a twelve string, was famously pictured being played by Jimi Hendrix and used as the image on a poster for the movie *See My Music Talking*.

Zemaitis came up with the idea of using metal to decorate instruments after shielding Fender Stratocaster pickups with metal to avoid the electrical hum for which the guitar was infamous. The next step was the creation of a series of metal-fronted electric guitars, each totally original, which by the early 1970s were to be seen in the hands of many leading rockers. The engravings on the metal panels were inspired by ornate shotguns Zemaitis had seen and admired, and each had its own distinctive look, thanks to the skills of gun engraver Danny O'Brien.

Full metal fronts were later joined by pearl and disc-fronted guitars, but all (save a brief Student series in 1980) were made to measure—a fact that restricted output. These originals have since become collectible and have been toted by more recent players from Guns N' Roses and the Black Crowes. The marque was put back in production by a Japanese-funded company in the current millennium, despite Zemaitis's passing away in 2002.

The exquisite detail etched onto the metal-fronted Zemaitis guitars in emulation of shotguns made them instant collectors items. This single-cutaway example is typical.

GLOSSARY

action Height of strings above the guitar's fingerboard. A low action makes it easy for a player to form notes and chords with his or her fretting hand, but it may compromise the instrument's tone and cause string buzzing. High action often improves and boosts the sound but can lead to playing difficulties.

active Guitars with active circuitry have volume and tone controls that offer an electronic boost ("gain") to the signals they process. Standard, passive guitar controls can provide only attenuation.

Alnico Type of magnet widely used in pickup manufacture. The name is derived from the magnet's constituent materials: aluminum, nickel, and cobalt.

arch-top guitar Guitar with top carved or pressed into an arched shape. Contrast with **flat-top guitar**.

back pickup Pickup mounted closest to the bridge, providing a cutting, treble-rich tone often favored for solo passages.

barre chords A type of guitar chord where one finger is used like a bar to hold down more than one string.

Bartolini pickup A brand of pickup; others include EMG or Seymour Duncan.

binding Strip(s) of wood, plastic, or other material decorating the edges of a guitar's body.

bout Most guitars have bodies shaped like a figure eight; the wider sections above and below the waist are referred to as the upper and lower bouts. Arch-top and flat-top guitars are frequently categorized by the maximum width of their lower bouts (17 inches, 18 inches, etc.).

bridge Unit mounted on the lower part of a guitar's top and fitted with one or more saddles of metal,

wood, or other materials. It sets the end of the strings' vibrating length (which begins at the nut) and can usually be adjusted to affect their height and intonation.

burl Naturally occurring knot in a piece of wood.

capo Device that can be attached to the neck of a guitar. It is used for temporarily shortening the strings and thus raising the pitch of the instrument.

carved top Arched guitar top either carved by hand or made by machine. Contrast with **pressed top**.

CNC Computer Numeric Control. A method of controlling high-precision machine tools with computers during guitar manufacture.

coil tap Circuit that converts a humbucking pickup to single-coil operation.

Custom-build Many guitar makers establish their name and reputation by building outlandish custom-made guitars for rich clientele. These can include seven- and eight-string guitars, twin- or triple-neck guitars, and even guitar-sitars. Hugh Manson is one example of an innovative guitar maker.

cutaway Incision in the upper part of the guitar body adjacent to the neck, allowing the player's fretting hand to reach the highest positions more easily. See **Florentine cutaway** and **Venetian cutaway**.

decal Name tag or other symbol or trademark applied to an instrument via a transfer or similar means. Most often seen on guitar headstocks.

double-tracking Studio technique allowing an artist to overdub an additional part onto an audio recording he or she has already made.

drone string Unfretted string tuned to a preset pitch. Found on harp guitars and sitars.

Electric Spanish Term used by Gibson (and some other manufacturers) for electric guitars designed to be played in the "traditional" position (held upright in the arms). The name (and the Gibson prefix ES) differentiates these instruments from electric Hawaiian guitars (given the EH prefix by Gibson), which are placed horizontally on the performer's lap and fretted with a steel bar.

electromagnetic pickup See **single-coil pickup** and **humbucker**.

feedback Howling or squealing effect caused when an electric instrument picks up its own amplified sound from a nearby loudspeaker. Some rock players deliberately induce feedback and use it as a musical tool.

f-hole Mimicking the sound holes of classical instruments, f-holes were first used in Rickenbacker guitars of the early 1930s, such as their Electro-Spanish model. They are seen on many hollow-bodied electric guitars from Gretsch and Gibson.

flat-top guitar Steel-strung guitar with a flat (that is, not arched) top.

flatwound Flatwound strings have either a round or hexagonal core, but the exterior winding wire is flatter giving a shallower profile than roundwound strings. They are more comfortable to play, reduce wear on frets and fretboards, and are significantly less "squeaky" than roundwound strings.

floating pickup Pickup that makes no contact with a guitar's top, thereby preserving the instrument's acoustic integrity. (Pickups mounted directly onto the top tend to deaden its vibrations, compromising the acoustic sound.)

Florentine cutaway Term used by Gibson to describe the sharp-horned cutaway seen on guitars such as the ES-175. Contrast with **Venetian cutaway**.

Frequensator Type of tailpiece designed by Epiphone and used on many of its arch-top guitars from the late 1930s onward. It has a double-trapeze shape and was intended to "equalize" treble and bass response by shortening the top three strings' path from bridge to tailpiece and by extending the length of the three lower strings.

fret Metal ridge inset across the fingerboard. Holding down a string behind a fret causes the string to be pressed against it, raising the pitch. Frets are positioned on the neck at intervals of a semitone

front pickup Pickup mounted closest to the neck, providing a warm, rounded tone often favored for chordal and rhythm playing.

full-body, full-depth Hollow-body electric guitar with a body depth (typically 3 inches) equivalent to that found on acoustic models.

harp-guitar Guitar with additional unfretted bass strings providing extended range. Developed by a number of late nineteenth and early twentieth century luthiers, notably Orville Gibson (1856–1918), and revived in a radically altered solid-body form by Californian luthier Steve Klein.

Hawaiian guitar Guitar designed to be played in a horizontal position on the performer's lap. Notes and chords are formed using a metal bar instead of the fingers of the fretting hand, permitting the rapid sliding up and down of the musical scale associated with Hawaiian guitar playing. The instrument's action is higher than a standard guitar's, and its neck profile is frequently square. Hawaiian guitars are also known as lap steels.

headstock Section of guitar neck above the nut. The tuning machines are mounted on it.

humbucker, humbucking pickup Twin-coil electromagnetic pickup invented by Gibson engineer Seth Lover (1910–1997). Like the single-coil pickup from which it was developed, the unit is mounted under a guitar's strings. As these are struck, they create variations in the pickup's magnetic field and generate electrical currents in its double coils; the resultant signal is amplified and fed to loudspeakers. One of the humbucking pickup's coils is wired out of phase with the other; this has the effect of canceling or helping to suppress—or "buck"—hum and noise.

impedance Electrical resistance, measured in ohms. Nearly all standard guitars and their amplifiers are high-impedance, while most professional recording equipment uses low-impedance circuitry, which is less susceptible to noise, interference, and high-frequency signal losses. The Gibson Les Paul Signature and the Les Paul Personal and Recording models all incorporate low-impedance pickups.

jack socket Insertion point for the jack plug that connects an electric guitar to an amplifier.

Kaoss pad A touchpad MIDI controller, sampler, and effects processor for musical instruments made by Korg.

laminate Material made by bonding together two or

more thin sheets of different woods or other constituents.

locking nut Type of nut often fitted to guitars with advanced vibrato units. It features bolts or other devices to prevent strings from going out of tune when the vibrato is used.

machine head See **tuning machine**.

Masonite Type of hardboard used in the construction of Danelectro guitars and replicas.

MIDI Musical Instrument Digital Interface. Standard protocol for the exchange of performance data between synthesizers, sequencers, and other digitally controlled devices. Some specially

equipped guitars can send and receive MIDI information.

neck-through-body construction Method of guitar construction in which a single piece of wood is used for the neck and the center section of the instrument's body.

nut Block of bone, ivory, ebony, metal, or synthetic material mounted at the headstock end of the neck. It sets the height and position of the strings as they pass through the grooved slots cut into it. It also acts like a fret, defining the start of the vibrating length of each open string (see **bridge**).

PAF Nickname for the world's first humbucking pickup manufactured by Gibson. When it was used on Gibson guitars, to protect the design, it came stamped with the initials P.A.F. (Patent Applied For). Even when it received its patent it continued to be known as a PAF.

parallel Pickup coils are normally wired in "series" (that is, with the same current flowing in turn through each of them). Some guitar makers equip their instruments with a switch to convert the pickups to "parallel," an electrical mode in which the same voltage is applied to each coil. This creates a thinner sound, somewhat similar to the effect of using a coil tap, but with the advantage that a parallel-switched humbucking pickup retains its noise-reducing capacity, as both its coils are still in circuit.

passive Standard guitar volume and tone controls are passive (or without active circuitry). They can reduce output level and attenuate higher frequencies but are unable to boost signals from the instrument's pickups.

phase The electrical polarity of one pickup relative to another. Pickups on some guitars can be switched out of phase, creating a distinctive, slightly hollow-sounding tone.

pick See **plectrum**.

pickguard Protective plate made of plastic, tortoiseshell, or other material, suspended (just below string height) above a guitar's top or screwed directly onto its body. It is designed to protect the instrument's finish from damage by stray plectrum strokes.

piezoelectric pickup A transducer that converts vibrations from a guitar body or bridge into electrical currents, which can then be amplified and fed to loudspeakers. Piezoelectric pickups provide a cleaner, more uncolored sound than electromagnetic pickups (see **humbucker** and **single-coil pickup**).

plectrum Thin, pointed piece of plastic, tortoiseshell, or other material, held between the thumb and forefinger of a guitarist's striking hand and used to pick or strum the instrument's strings.

potentiometer Sometimes known as a "pot," it is conventionally a three-terminal resistor used to control volume.

pressed top Arched guitar top pressed into shape (using heat or other means) instead of being carved out. Contrast with **carved top**.

purfling See **binding**.

Res-o-lectric unit Unit carrying a pickup and its associated wiring, designed by National in the

1930s to allow the firm's resonator guitars to be converted to electric operation.

resonator guitar Guitar originally developed by John Dopyera (1893–1988), fitted with one or more metal resonator assemblies. These instruments were manufactured by the National and Dobro companies, which merged in 1935.

reverse body Design where the instrument's treble wing, or "horn," is larger or higher than the one on its opposite (bass) side.

roundwound The simplest and cheapest guitar strings are roundwound. They have a round or hexagonal core and round-winding wire around the outside. The bumpiness of the spiral cross-section causes more friction than flatwound or halfwound strings.

saddle Platform made from wood, metal, or other material, mounted on (or forming part of) the bridge of the guitar at the point where the strings pass across it. Many electric guitar bridges feature individually adjustable saddles for each string.

scratchplate See **pickguard**.

semi-acoustic guitar A guitar fitted with one or more electromagnetic pickups but also featuring a hollow body and some degree of acoustic sound.

semi-solid guitar Guitar combining a solid construction (usually at its center) with hollow body cavities. The most famous example is probably the Gibson ES-335.

series See **parallel**.

Signature guitar A specially produced custom version of a standard guitar as played by one of the great guitarists. The signature guitar will contain all the modifications and adaptations of the original, including the artwork. With some famously well-used guitars even the wear marks are included.

single-coil pickup Electromagnetic pickup fitted with a single coil (as opposed to the humbucker's twin coils) and mounted beneath a guitar's strings. Their vibrations create variations in the pickup's magnetic field and generate electrical currents in the coil; these are amplified and fed to loudspeakers.

solid body Electric guitar with no resonating cavities, constructed from a solid slab (or glued-together pieces) of wood.

sound hole(s) Hole(s), normally round, oval, or f-shaped, cut into a guitar's top. Their original purpose was to project the instrument's acoustic sound, but on many electric instruments their function is chiefly or exclusively decorative. Some Gretsch "Chet Atkins" models have a sealed top (to reduce the risk of feedback) with fake, painted-on f-holes.

stop tailpiece, stud tailpiece Metal block-type tailpiece found on many solid and semi-solid electrics. Unlike the more traditional hinged trapeze tailpiece, the "stud" or "stop" unit is attached to the body a little way below the bridge.

sunburst (finish) Classic guitar finish. At the center of the guitar is an area of lighter color, usually gold, that darkens gradually to brown toward the edges, merging into a black rim.

sustain block Also known as a tremolo block, it can be made of steel, tungsten, or titanium.

Superstrat Solid guitar with a shape roughly similar to the Fender Stratocaster but fitted with more powerful pickups and a vibrato unit, as well as other "hot rod" features.

tailpiece Metal or wooden fitting installed below a guitar's bridge and acting as an anchor for its string ends. Traditional arch-top guitar-style tailpieces (also seen on some solid-body instruments), are often hinged and in a trapeze shape. Later, units such as the stop or stud tailpiece became popular with many makers and players.

thinline Arch-top electric guitar with reduced depth (typically 1.75 inches) compared with its acoustic counterparts.

top The "face" of the guitar; its uppermost body surface, with pickups, bridge, and other parts mounted on it. The tops of semi-acoustic and many semi-solid instruments feature sound holes and bracing on their undersides.

transducer An electrical device used to produce an electrical signal from an acoustic guitar.

tremolo arm, tremolo unit, "trem" See **vibrato unit**.

truss rod Metal bar inserted into a guitar neck to improve its strength and rigidity. Most electric guitars have adjustable truss rods whose tension can be changed to correct bowing or warping in the neck.

tuning machine Geared string-tuning mechanism mounted in the guitar's headstock.

Underwound pickup An overwound pickup has relatively more windings of copper wire around the pole pieces—anywhere from 2 to 5 percent more wire—than a standard, stock pickup. An underwound pickup has fewer windings in about the same proportion. Underwound pickups produce a milder, less forceful sound that many rhythm guitar players prefer.

Venetian cutaway Term used by Gibson to describe the rounded-horn cutaway seen on guitars such as the ES-5. Contrast with **Florentine cutaway**.

vibrato unit, vibrato arm Mechanical device, usually attached to or built into a guitar's tailpiece, that allows the player to create pitch bends by loosening or tightening the instrument's strings with a lever or arm. *Vibrato* is the musical term for rapid pitch fluctuation, while tremolo is the effect produced by a series of fast repetitions of the same note. Therefore, "vibrato unit" is the correct name for pitch-bending devices of this kind, although many manufacturers and players refer to them as "tremolos" or "trems."

Vibrola Type of vibrato unit invented by Clayton O. ("Doc") Kauffman and used on many Rickenbacker guitars.

whammy bar Nickname (used by rock guitarists) for a vibrato or tremolo arm.

Wildwood Type of dyed wood produced in Scandinavia and used by Fender on some of its instruments.

X-bracing Method of strengthening the tops of guitars and controlling or modifying their tonal characteristics by using struts crossed in an "X" pattern. It was first popularized by C.F. Martin (1786–1873), and it has become a standard method of bracing for flat-top and some arch-top designs.

INDEX

Picture Credits